JAPANESE PICTURE DICTIONARY COLORING BOOK

Over 1500 Japanese Words and Phrases for Creative & Visual Learners of All Ages

Color and Learn

ISBN-13: 978-1-951949-61-7

Free Book Reveals The 6 Step Blueprint That Took Students **From Language Learners To Fluent In 3 Months**

- **6 Unbelievable Hacks** that will accelerate your learning curve

- **Mind Training:** why memorizing vocabulary is easy

- **One Hack To Rule Them All:** This <u>secret nugget</u> will blow you away...

Head over to **LingoMastery.com/hacks** and claim your free book now!

CONTENTS

INTRODUCTION

This Japanese Picture Dictionary Coloring Book has been designed to help new learners of the Japanese language to build vocabulary in the most fun and relaxing way. This book aims to teach basic Japanese grammar rules with potentially colorful and exciting exercises. It covers an immense range of topics that will help you learn everything related to the Japanese language for day-to-day living. For example, animal names, family, body parts, emotions, seasons and other items around us.

You will find there are many fascinating illustrations based on the vocabulary you learn on each page. The fun part is that you can color the illustrations while learning. You no longer have to make hundreds of boring flash cards to memorize Japanese vocabulary thanks to this great language learning tool in your hands. Get your coloring pencils ready and let's learn some Japanese vocabulary together!

BASICS OF THE JAPANESE LANGUAGE

I.   Japanese characters

The Japanese language has three types of characters: hiragana, katakana and kanji.

a. Hiragana

1) 46 hiragana characters

Hiragana is a phonetic alphabetic system that is mainly used for native Japanese words, conjugating verbs, and grammatical particles. A total of 46 hiragana characters is used in the Japanese writing system.

あ	い	う	え	お
a	i	u	e	o
か	き	く	け	こ
ka	ki	ku	ke	ko
さ	し	す	せ	そ
sa	shi	su	se	so
た	ち	つ	て	と
ta	chi	tsu	te	to
な	に	ぬ	ね	の
na	ni	nu	ne	no
は	ひ	ふ	へ	ほ
ha (wa)	hi	fu	he (e)	ho
ま	み	む	め	も
ma	mi	mu	me	mo
や		ゆ		よ
ya		yu		yo
ら	り	る	れ	ろ
ra	ri	ru	re	ro
わ				を
wa				wo
ん				
n				

3

2) Hiragana with diacritical marks

Additionally, hiragana makes use of two diacritical marks. The two small dashes (゛) are called dakuten (濁点). The small circle (゜) is called handakuten (半濁点). By adding these diacritical marks onto the hiragana characters, you can change the sound of the character. With the dakuten (゛), the consonants *k, s, t, h* become the consonants *g, z, d, b*, respectively. The consonant *h* changes to a *p* sound with handakuten (゜). Look at the chart below.

が	ぎ	ぐ	げ	ご
ga	gi	gu	ge	go
ざ	じ	ず	ぜ	ぞ
za	ji	zu	ze	zo
だ	ぢ	づ	で	ど
da	ji	zu	de	do
ば	び	ぶ	べ	ぼ
ba	bi	bu	be	bo
ぱ	ぴ	ぷ	ぺ	ぽ
pa	pi	pu	pe	po

3) Contracted sounds

When the hiragana characters や, ゆ and よ are written in smaller size, they take on a new function, transcribing contracted sounds. In the chart below, you will see all hiragana characters with the small や, ゆ and よ.

きゃ	きゅ	きょ
kya	kyu	kyo
しゃ	しゅ	しょ
sha	shu	sho
ちゃ	ちゅ	ちょ
cha	chu	cho
にゃ	にゅ	にょ
nya	nyu	nyo
ひゃ	ひゅ	ひょ
hya	hyu	hyo
みゃ	みゅ	みょ

mya	myu	myo
りゃ	りゅ	りょ
rya	ryu	ryo
びゃ	びゅ	びょ
bya	byu	byo
ぴゃ	ぴゅ	ぴょ
pya	pyu	pyo
ぎゃ	ぎゅ	ぎょ
gya	gyu	gyo
じゃ	じゅ	じょ
ja	ju	jo

4) Double consonants (small "tsu")

When the hiragana character つ is written in smaller size and is inserted between two characters, this creates a different sound and indicates that the first letter of very next character should be doubled. See some examples below.

きっぷ *kippu* (ticket)
はっぱ *happa* (leaf)
ざっし *zasshi* (magazine)

b. Katakana

1) 46 katakana characters

Katakana is also a phonetic alphabetic system. It has 46 corresponding characters which make the same sounds as found in hiragana. But the main difference is that katakana is used for loanwords and foreign names.

ア	イ	ウ	エ	オ
a	i	u	e	o
カ	キ	ク	ケ	コ
ka	ki	ku	ke	ko
サ	シ	ス	セ	ソ
sa	shi	su	se	so
タ	チ	ツ	テ	ト
ta	chi	tsu	te	to
ナ	ニ	ヌ	ネ	ノ
na	ni	nu	ne	no
ハ	ヒ	フ	ヘ	ホ
ha (wa)	hi	fu	he (e)	ho
マ	ミ	ム	メ	モ
ma	mi	mu	me	mo
ヤ		ユ		ヨ
ya		yu		yo
ラ	リ	ル	レ	ロ
ra	ri	ru	re	ro
ワ				ヲ
wa				wo
ン				
n				

2) Katakana with diacritical marks

In the chart below, you will see all 25 katakana characters with diacritical marks and the corresponding letters of the alphabet.

ガ	ギ	グ	ゲ	ゴ
ga	gi	gu	ge	go
ザ	ジ	ズ	ゼ	ゾ
za	ji	zu	ze	zo
ダ	ヂ	ヅ	デ	ド
da	ji	zu	de	do
バ	ビ	ブ	ベ	ボ
ba	bi	bu	be	bo
パ	ピ	プ	ペ	ポ
pa	pi	pu	pe	po

3) Katakana contracted sounds

You will see all katakana contracted sounds in the chart below. The pronunciations are the same as in hiragana.

キャ	キュ	キョ
kya	kyu	kyo
シャ	シュ	ショ
sha	shu	sho
チャ	チュ	チョ
cha	chu	cho
ニャ	ニュ	ニョ
nya	nyu	nyo
ヒャ	ヒュ	ヒョ
hya	hyu	hyo
ミャ	ミュ	ミョ

mya	myu	myo
リャ	リュ	リョ
rya	ryu	ryo
ギャ	ギュ	ギョ
gya	gyu	gyo
ジャ	ジュ	ジョ
ja	ju	jo
ビャ	ビュ	ビョ
bya	byu	byo
ピャ	ピュ	ピョ
pya	pyu	pyo

4) The long vowels

The long vowel sounds are written with a dash (—) called a Chōon (長音) mark in katakana. See the examples below.

ツアー *tsuaa* (tour)
スーツ *suutsu* (suit)
スキー *sukii* (ski)

c. Kanji

Kanji characters are actually Chinese characters that were introduced to Japan back when the Japanese language did not yet have its own writing system. Kanji represents both meanings and sounds. Many of them are made from pictures of objects. There are four categories of kanji and they reference the way characters originally came to be: *Pictograph, Indicator, Compound ideographs and Phonetic ideographic characters.* See the example below.

1. Pictograph: Kanji characters that originated from pictures of objects.

Example: 木 (tree), 山 (mountain), 川 (river)

2. Indicator: These kanji characters translate abstract concepts into symbols.

Example: 一 (one), 上 (top), 下 (bottom)

3. Compound ideographs: This category of kanji is formed by combining two or more existing kanji characters.

Example: 日 (sun) + 月 (moon) = 明 (bright)

4. Phonetic ideographic characters: Kanji made up of one-part sound and one-part meaning.

Example: ⺾ (grass: meaning) + 化 (ka: sound) = 花(flower)

> **How to read kanji characters**

There are two different ways to read kanji characters. The first way to read it is with the original Chinese pronunciation called on-reading (*on-yomi*) and the second is kun-reading (*kun-yomi*) which is the Japanese pronunciation for the same character.

See the example below.

日 Sun, day	On-reading	Kun-reading
	に、にち	ひ、び、か

月 Moon, month	On-reading	Kun-reading
	げつ、がつ	つき

7

> ➤ **Furigana**

To show how kanji characters are intended to be read in the context, hiragana characters are sometimes provided. These hiragana characters are called furigana. Furigana is placed either above or next to kanji characters. This is especially helpful for children and learners of the Japanese language. Another function of furigana is to clarify rare kanji readings. See the example below.

かんじ　おぼ　　　　　むずか
漢字を覚えるのは 難 しい。

As shown above, furigana is added right above all the kanji characters. The same method is used throughout this book to assist learners in studying kanji in its context and its reading.

Japanese Grammar

I. Personal pronouns

The term わたし(watashi) or ぼく (boku) is used to refer to yourself. While *watashi* is a genderless and formal personal pronoun that can be used in business settings, *boku* sounds more casual and is used only by men. In Japanese, the second person pronoun "you" is *anata*. The third person pronoun "he" is *kare* and the pronoun "she" is *kanojo*. However, Japanese native speakers don't use these personal pronouns too often. Rather than using these personal pronouns, native speakers prefer using their own names in conversation.

In the case of pluralizing personal pronouns, simply add たち after each personal pronoun.

Singular		Plural	
わたし	I (both men and women)	わたしたち	we
ぼく	I (only for men)	ぼくたち	we
あなた	you	あなたたち	you
かれ	he	かれら	plural for he
かのじょ	she	かのじょたち	plural for she

II. X is/isn't Y

First, let's learn the most basic structure of the Japanese language. "I am Shinji", "That is my car", "I am American." These sentences, which don't contain verbs, can be formed by using the following grammar pattern.

X is Y	X は Y です
X isn't Y	X は Y じゃないです/じゃありません/ではありません

There are mainly three variations of the negative form: the first form: じゃないです is casual and colloquial, The second one: じゃありません is formal. The last one; ではありません is appropriate for writing.

Example:

わたしはしんじです。 *Watashi wa Shinji desu*　　　I am Shinji.

わたしはアメリカ人じゃありません。 *Watashi wa amerikajin ja arimasen*　 I am not American.

Important Note: "a", "an" and "the" doesn't exist in Japanese.

The past tense of the sentence *X is/isn't Y* is demonstrated below. In the box below, you will notice that the auxiliary verb です is replaced with the past tense form of that verb でした. You will also notice that the negative form じゃないです is replaced with じゃなかったです.

X was Y	X は Y でした
X wasn't Y	X は Y じゃなかったです

You can also use a fomal variant じゃありませんでした instead of じゃなかったです. For writing, ではありませんでした is appropriate to use.

III. Verbs

a. Present tense

Japanese is a Subject-Object-Verb (SOV) language, which means that the verb always goes at the end. Unlike English, pronouns and subjects can be omitted if it is clear from the context. Please see below an example of the correct sentence order in Japanese.

Sentence order: Subject ＋ Object ＋ Verb

Example：わたしは 音楽を聴きます。

I listen to music.

9

There are three kinds of verbs in Japanese. The first group of verbs are called ru-verbs. The second group is called u-verbs. The third group is called irregular verbs.

1) Group 1: ru-verbs

Japanese verbs always contain two parts: a verb base and a suffix. The ru-verbs always start with the base and end with the suffix *ru*. In the example below, the verb *tabe* (to eat) is the base and *ru* is a suffix.

For affirmative and negative verbs, there is a short form and a long form. Short forms are used in casual conversations.

Plain Form	Affirmative	Negative
たべる	たべる / たべます	たべない / たべません
taberu	taberu / tabemasu	tabenai / tabemasen

Summary

- **The long form:** For affirmative, replace る(*ru*) with the suffix *masu* and for negative, *masen*.
- **The short form:** For negative, replace る(*ru*) with the suffix *nai*.

2) Group 2: u-verb

The u-verbs start with the verb base and end with the suffix *u*. The example below illustrates how to conjugate u-verbs.

Plain Form	Affirmative	Negative
のむ	のむ / のみます	のまない / のみません
nomu	nomu / nomimasu	nomanai / nomimasen

Summary

- **The long form:** For affirmative, replace *u* with the suffix *imasu* and for negative, *imasen*.
- **The short form:** For negative, replace *u* with the suffix *anai*.
- If a verb ends with the hiragana character う, replace う with the suffix *wanai*.

3) Group 3: Irregular verb

There are two irregular verbs. They do not follow the conjugation patterns in group 1 or group 2 as discussed above.

Plain Form	Affirmative	Negative
する	する / します	しない / しません
suru	**suru / shimasu**	**shinai / shimasen**
くる	くる / きます	こない / きません
kuru	**kuru / kimasu**	**konai / kimasen**

Another factor that is worth remembering is that the "present tense" you learned in this section can be used for; (1) the activities that a person habitually or regularly engages in, (2) the activities that a person will do in the future. Therefore the "present tense" of the verbs here are not only used for the present tense but also for the future tense.

b. Past tense

To conjugate a verb for the past tense affirmative form, we simply add the suffix *mashita* instead of *masu*. For the negative form, the suffix *deshita* will be added after *masen*. See the example below.

	Affirmative		Negative	
	Present	Past	Present	Past
ru-verb	たべます	たべました	たべません	たべませんでした
u-verb	のみます	のみました	のみません	のみませんでした
Irregular verb	します	しました	しません	しませんでした

IV. Adjectives

There are two groups of adjectives in Japanese. Group 1 is called い-adjective and group 2 is called な-adjective. These two groups of adjectives follow different conjugation patterns. Unlike in English, you also need to conjugate adjectives depending on the tense, whether it be present or past tense.

1) Group 1: い-adjective

All adjectives in this group end with い. The example below shows how to conjugate い-adjective.

Plain form	Present		Past	
	Affirmative	Negative	Affirmative	Negative
おいしい tasty	おいしい	おいしくない	おいしかった	おいしくなかった

To sound more polite, add the auxiliary verb です after these adjectives (affirmative and negative).

Basic Conjugation Rules of the い- adjectives

- For the negative present tense form, replace い with くない
- For the affirmative past tense form, replace い with かった
- For the negative past tense form, replace い with くなかった

Example:

おいしい食事　*Oishii shokuji*　Tasty meal
なっとうはおいしくなかった。　*Nattou wa oishikunakatta*　Natto wasn't tasty.

There is only one important exception. Please note below.

Plain form	Present		Past	
	Affirmative	Negative	Affirmative	Negative
いい good	いい	よくない	よかった	よくなかった

Another adjective that conjugates like this is かっこいい which means handsome. If you look closely at this adjective, you will find いい inside the adjective. Therefore, you need to use the same conjugation.

2) Group 2: な-adjective

All adjectives in this group end with な. The example below shows how to conjugate な-adjective.

Plain form	Present		Past	
	Affirmative	Negative	Affirmative	Negative
きれいな beautiful	きれいです	きれいじゃないで す	きれいでし た	きれいじゃなかっ たです

Basic Conjugation Rules of the な-adjectives

- For the affirmative present form, replace な with です
- For the negative present form, replace な with じゃないです
- For the affirmative past form, replace な with でした
- For the negative past form, replace な with じゃなかったです

Example:

きれいな公園　*Kireina kouen*　Beautiful park

公園はきれいでした。　*Kouen wa kirei deshita*　The park was beautiful.

V. Particle

Nouns in sentences are followed by one or two hiragana characters which is called the "particle." Each particle indicates how the word before it relates to other words in the sentence, usually to the verb. See the list of particles you will learn in this section.

Purpose	Particle
Topic	は
Direct object	を
Location and means	で
Time and goal of movement	に
Goal of movement	へ
Origin	から
Co-participant	と
Possession	の

1) は: Topic Particle

The most important particle is the topic particle: は. When it is used as a particle, it is pronounced "*wa*." The topic particle identifies the topic of the sentence. It can be translated as "as for" or "speaking of" in English. See the examples below.

Example:

わたしは日本人です。　*Watashi wa nihonjin desu*　I am Japanese.

今日は雨です。　*Kyou wa ame desu*　As for today, it is rainy.

2) を：Object particle

The particle を indicates the object of the verb which can be a person or a thing that, that action is done to. See the examples below.

Example:

コーヒーを飲みます。　*Koohii wo nomimasu*　I drink coffee.

すしを食べます。　*Sushi wo tabemasu*　I eat sushi.

3) で：Location and the means particle

The particle で indicates where the event takes place. In English, it can be translated "in" or "at". This particle is also used to describe the means of transportation and what is used to carry it out. In this case, the English equivalent is "by" or "with." See the example below.

Example：

家で本を読みます。　*Ie de hon wo yomimasu*　I read books at home. (Location)

タクシーで新宿に行きます。　*Takushii de shinjuku ni ikimasu*　I go to Shinjuku by taxi. (Means)

4) に：Goal of movement and time

This particle is mainly used to indicate time and goal of movement.

Example:

ジョンはアメリカに帰りました。*Jon wa america ni kaerimashita.*　John returned to the United States.

朝6時に起きました。　*Asa rokuji ni okimashita*　I woke up at 6 in the morning.

日曜日に浅草に行きます。　*Nichiyoubi ni Asakusa ni ikimasu*　I will go to Asakusa on Sunday.

14

5) へ： Goal of movement

The particle へ also indicates the goal of movement. But this particle cannot be used to identify time as particle に.

Example:

あした がっこう　い
明日 学 校へ行きます。 *Ashita gakkou he ikimasu* I will go to school tomorrow.

6) から： Origin

The particle から indicates the starting point of something or where something comes from.

Example：

じ　　はたら
8時から 働 きます。 *Hachiji kara hatarakimasu* I work from 8 o'clock.
き
イギリスから来ました。 *Igirisu kara kimashita* I came from the U.K.

7) と： Co-participant

The particle と mainly has two functions. First, it can be used to connect two nouns in a list. In English it is similar to the joining word "and." Second, it is used to describe with whom you do something.

Example:

えいご　　　ご　はな
サンディは英語とスペイン語を 話します。 *Sandy wa eigo to supeingo wo hanashimasu*
Sandy speaks English and Spanish.
てん　　　た
すしと天 ぷらを食べました。 *Sushi to tenpura wo tabemashita*
I ate sushi and tempura.
とも　　　とうきょう　い
友だちと東 京 に行きました。 *Tomodachi to Tokyo ni ikimashita*
I went to Tokyo with my friend.

8) の : Possession

The particle の connects two nouns. One of the main ways to use this particle is to indicate possession. It acts like the possessive "s" or "of" in English. However, this particle has more functions. See the example below.

Example:

わたしの 車 　*Watashi no kuruma* 　My car

ゴッホの絵 　*Gohho no e* 　Gogh's painting

日本の学校 　*Nihon no gakkou* 　A school in Japan

木のつくえ 　*Ki no tsukue* 　A wooden desk

The role of this particle may look complicated. But keep in mind that the main idea comes at the end and the first noun gives more information about the second noun.

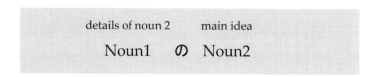

details of noun 2 　　 main idea

Noun1 　の 　Noun2

VI. Japanese Sentence Structure

In Japanese, the word order is quite flexible. The only rule that has to be adhered to is that verbs always come last. However, the topic and the time phrases are often placed at the beginning of sentences. Please see the example below.

わたしは	金曜日に	学校で	日本語を	勉強します。
topic	time	place	object	verb

I study Japanese on Friday at school.

VII. Question Sentences

To form question sentences in Japanese, you simply need to add か(*ka*) at the end of each sentence. Take note that it is not very common to write the question mark at the end of a question sentence in Japanese.

16

ジョンはアメリカ人です。 *Jon wa america jin desu* John is American.

ジョンはアメリカ人ですか。 *Jon wa america jin desuka* Is John American?

Question sentences may contain question words such as what, where, when, why, who and which. See the list of Japanese question words.

Question words	Japanese
What	何（なに、なん）
Where	どこ
When	いつ
Why	なぜ、どうして
Who	だれ
Which	どっち、どれ
How much	いくら

Basically, the following pattern is used to ask questions with a question word. See the example sentences below.

$$\boxed{\text{Object}} \quad は \quad \boxed{\text{Question word}} \quad ですか。$$

1) What – 何（なん、なに）

The question word "what" in Japanese has two pronunciations: *nani* and *nan*. *Nani* is usually used before a particle and *nan* is used right before the auxiliary verb *desu* or before a counter such as *ji* (o'clock) and *sai* (age). Therefore, *nan-sai* means "how old" and *nan-ji* means "what time."

これは何ですか。 *Kore wa nan desuka*
What is this?

今、何時ですか。 *Ima nanji desuka*
What time is it now?

何が好きですか。 *Nani ga suki desuka*
What do you like?

17

2) Where – どこ

The question word どこ is used to ask for a location when you are traveling.

トイレは<u>どこ</u>ですか。　*Toire wa doko desuka*
Where is the bathroom?

3) When – いつ

A question word いつ is used to ask for "when."

<ruby>誕<rt>たん</rt></ruby><ruby>生<rt>じょう</rt></ruby><ruby>日<rt>び</rt></ruby>は<u>いつ</u>ですか。　*Tanjoubi wa itsu desuka*
When is your birthday?

4) Why – なぜ、どうして

There are few ways to ask "why" in Japanese. The first one, なぜ is used in formal writing and speech but not in daily conversation. The second one, どうして sounds more casual and is used in everyday conversation.

<ruby>苦<rt>くる</rt></ruby>しみがこれほど<ruby>多<rt>おお</rt></ruby>いのは<u>なぜ</u>ですか。*Kurushimi ga korehodo ooi nowa naze desuka*
Why is there so much suffering?

<u>どうして</u><ruby>仕事<rt>しごと</rt></ruby>をやめたんですか。　*Doushite Shigoto wo yametandesuka*
Why did you quit the job?

5) Who – だれ

The question word for who is だれ and for the possessive question word "whose" the particle の is used after the question word.

あの<ruby>人<rt>ひと</rt></ruby>は<u>だれ</u>ですか。　*Ano hito wa dare desuka*
Who is that person?

<u>だれ</u>のかさですか？　*Dare no kasa desuka*
Whose umbrella is this?

6) Which – どっち、どれ

When there are only two options, the question word どっち is used. If more than two options are available, the question word どれ is used.

どっちが好きですか。　*Docchi ga suki desuka*
Which do you like more?

この中でどれが一番好きですか。　*Kono naka de dore ga ichiban suki desuka*
Which do you like the best among these?

7) How much – いくら

The question word いくら is used to ask for the price of something.

この時計はいくらですか？　*Kono tokei wa ikura desuka*
How much is this watch?

Final Note: This chapter covers an overview of the basic Japanese grammar rules. This will certainly help you understand the basic Japanese sentence structure as you continue to learn Japanese using this book. However, this section is just a simple introduction and doesn't cover more than the basics. For in-depth grammar explanations, we recommend that you visit our website where there is a variety of options of Japanese books for further learning. In Japanese, we say *Ganbatte!* がんばって！that translates to "All the best!"

感情 (EMOTIONS)

1) 嬉しい (happy)
   ureshii

2) 悲しい (sad)
   kanashii

3) ワクワクする (excited)
   wakuwaku suru

4) 怒る (angry)
   okoru

5) 驚く (surprised)
   odoroku

6) 心配する (concerned)
   shinpaisuru

7) 怖がる (scared)
   kowagaru

8) 気になる (curious)
   kininaru

9) 面白い (amused)
   omoshiroi

10) 混乱する (confused)
    konransuru

11) 病気になる (sick)
    byouki ni naru

12) わんぱくな (naughty)
    wanpakuna

13) 真面目な (serious)
    majimena

14) 集中する (focused)
    shuuchuusuru

15) 退屈な (bored)
    taikutsuna

16) 圧倒される (overwhelmed)
    attousareru

17) 恋をする (to be in love)
    koi wo suru

18) 恥ずかしい (ashamed)
    hazukashii

19) 不安になる (anxious)
    fuanninaru

20) むかつく (disgusted)
    mukatsuku

21) 腹を立てる (offended)
    harawotateru

22) 傷つく (sore)
    kizutsuku

とても嬉しいです。 *Totemo ureshii desu.*
I am very happy.

仕事に集中します。 *Shigoto ni shuuchuu shimasu.*
I focus on the work.

20

かぞく
家族 (THE FAMILY)

1) そふぼ
   祖父母 (grandparents)
   sofubo

2) おばあちゃん / 祖母 (grandmother) そぼ
   obaachan / sobo

3) おじいちゃん / 祖父 (grandfather) そふ
   ojiichan / sofu

4) おじさん / 叔父 (uncle) おじ
   ojisan / oji

5) お母さん / 母 (mother) かあ はは
   okaasan / haha

6) お父さん / 父 (father) とう ちち
   otousan / chichi

7) おばさん / 叔母 (aunt) おば
   obasan / oba

8) いとこ (cousin)
   itoko

9) きょうだい
   兄弟 (brothers, sisters)
   kyoudai

10) わたし ぼく
    私 / 僕 (me)
    watashi / boku

11) おっと つま
    夫 / 妻 (husband/wife)
    otto / tsuma

12) しまい
    姉妹 (sisters)
    shimai

13) いとこ (cousin)
    itoko

14) おい (nephew)
    oi

15) むすこ
    息子 (son)
    Musuko

16) むすめ
    娘 (daughter)
    musume

17) めい (niece)
    mei

18) まごむすこ
    孫息子 (grandson)
    mago musuko

19) まごむすめ
    孫娘 (granddaughter)
    mago musume

20) はとこ (second cousin)
    hatoko

• ぎり かぞく しんせき
  義理の家族 (in-laws) – 親戚 (relatives)
  giri no kazoku – shinseki

21) ぎり ちち
    義理の父 (father-in-law)
    giri no chichi

22) ぎり はは
    義理の母 (mother-in-law)
    giri no haha

23) ぎり きょうだい
    義理の兄弟 (brother-in-law)
    giri no kyoudai

24) ぎり しまい
    義理の姉妹 (sister-in-law)
    giri no shimai

25) ぎり むすめ
    義理の娘 (daughter-in-law)
    giri no musume

26) ぎり むすこ
    義理の息子 (son-in-law)
    giri no musuko

27) ぎり おじ
    義理の叔父 (uncle-in-law)
    giri no oji

28) ぎり おば
    義理の叔母 (aunt-in-law)
    giri no oba

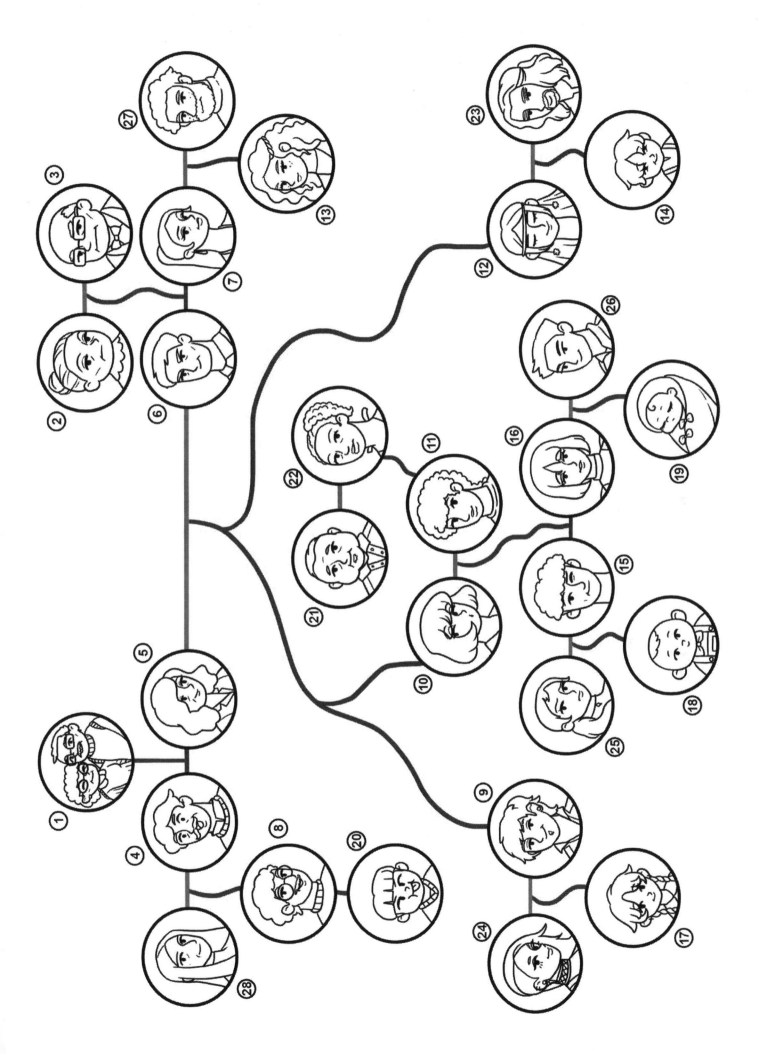

関係 (RELATIONSHIPS)

1) 夫婦 (married couple)
   fuufu

2) 既婚男性 (married man)
   kikon dansei

3) 既婚女性 (married woman)
   kikon josei

4) 離婚した夫婦 (divorced couple)
   rikonshita fuufu

5) 前の妻 (ex-wife)
   mae no tsuma

6) 前の夫 (ex-husband)
   mae no otto

7) 友達 (friend)
   tomodachi

8) 彼女 (girlfriend)
   kanojo

9) 彼氏 (boyfriend)
   kareshi

10) 近所の人 (neighbor)
    kinjo no hito

11) 独身 (single)
    dokushin

12) 離婚女性 / 離婚男性
    (divorcée/divorcé)
    rikon josei / rikon dansei

13) 寡夫 (widower)
    kafu

14) 未亡人 (widow)
    miboujin

新しい彼氏ができました。 *Atarashii kareshi ga dekimashita.*
I got a new boyfriend.

私はまだ独身です。 *Watashi wa mada dokushin desu.*
I am still single.

友達と富士山を見に行きます。 *Tomodachi to fujisan wo mini ikimasu.*
I'll go to see Mt. Fuji with friends.

24

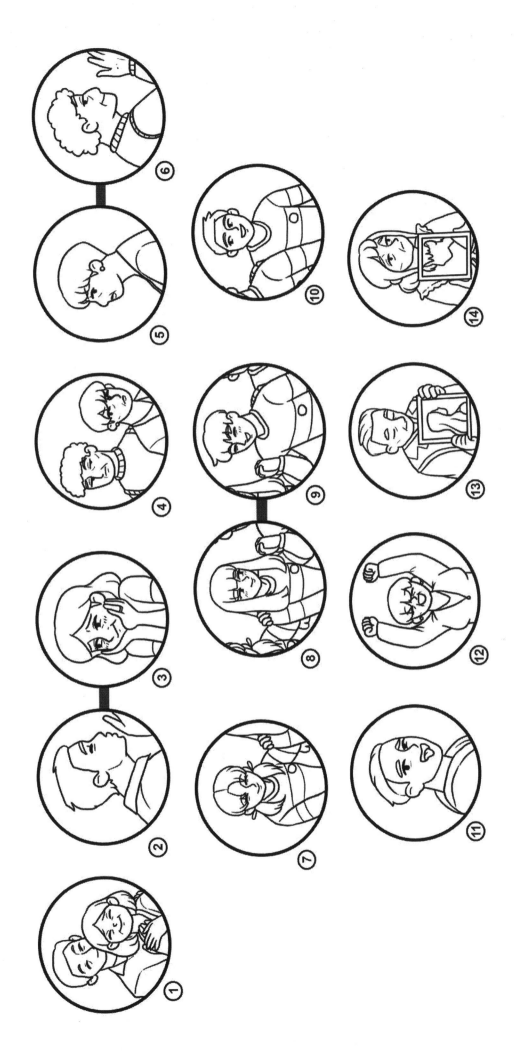

価値 (VALUES)

かち

1) 尊敬 (respect)
そんけい
sonkei

2) 感謝 (gratitude)
かんしゃ
kansha

3) 寛容 (tolerance)
かんよう
kanyou

4) 協力 (collaboration)
きょうりょく
kyouryoku

5) 正直 (honesty)
しょうじき
shoujiki

6) 禁酒 (temperance)
きんしゅ
kinshu

7) 責任 (responsibility)
せきにん
sekinin

8) 信仰 (faith)
しんこう
shinkou

9) 勇気 (courage)
ゆうき
yuuki

10) 親切 (kindness)
しんせつ
shinsetsu

11) 献身 (commitment)
けんしん
kenshin

12) 熱意 (enthusiasm)
ねつい
netsui

13) 信頼 (trust)
しんらい
shinrai

14) 時間厳守 (punctuality)
じかんげんしゅ
jikan genshu

たが　　かんしゃ
お互いに感謝しましょう。*Otagaini kansha shimashou.*
Show gratitude to each other.

しんらい
あなたを信頼しています。*Anata wo shinrai shiteimasu.*
I trust you.

しごと　せきにん　おも
仕事の責任が重いです。*Shigoto no sekinin ga omoidesu.*
My responsibility at work is heavy.

人体 (THE HUMAN BODY)

1) 頭 (head)
atama

2) 髪の毛 / 髪 (hair)
kami no ke / kami

3) 顔 (face)
kao

4) おでこ (forehead)
odeko

5) 耳 (ear)
mimi

6) 目 (eyes)
me

7) 鼻 (nose)
hana

8) ほっぺた / 頬 (cheek)
hoppeta / hoho

9) 口 (mouth)
kuchi

10) あご (chin)
ago

11) 首 (neck)
kubi

12) 背中 (back)
senaka

13) 胸 (chest)
mune

14) 肩 (shoulder)
kata

15) 腕 (arm)
ude

16) 前腕 (forearm)
zenwan

17) 手 (hand)
te

18) おなか (stomach, belly)
onaka

19) 腰 (waist)
koshi

20) お尻 (hip)
oshiri

21) 足 (leg)
ashi

22) もも (thigh)
momo

23) 膝 (knee)
hiza

24) ふくらはぎ (calf)
fukurahagi

25) すね (shin)
sune

26) 脚 (leg, foot)
ashi

7才のとき、腕の骨を折った。 *Nana sai no toki ude no hone wo otta.*
I broke my arm when I was 7.

まだ背中が痛いですか。 *Mada senaka ga itai desuka.*
Does your back still hurt?

28

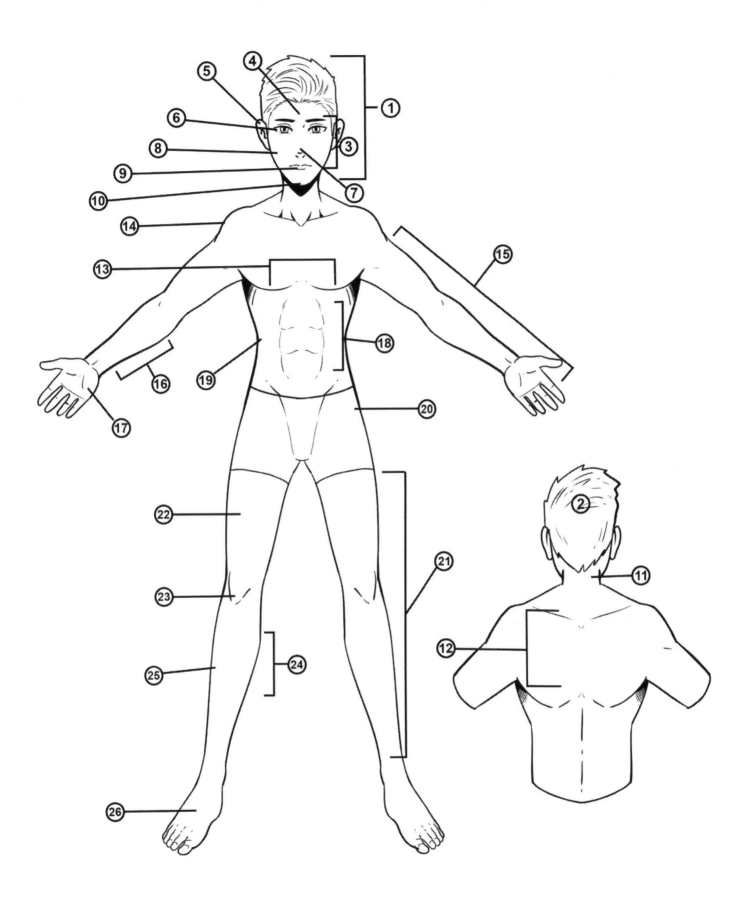

人体の内部 (INSIDE THE HUMAN BODY)

1) 肌 (skin)
hada

2) 筋肉 (muscle)
kinniku

3) 骨 (bone)
hone

4) 脳 (brain)
nou

5) 甲状腺 (thyroid)
koujousen

6) 血管 (vein)
kekkan

7) 動脈 (artery)
doumyaku

8) 心臓 (heart)
shinzou

9) 肺 (lung)
hai

10) 胃 (stomach)
i

11) 食道 (esophagus)
shokudou

12) すい臓 (pancreas)
souizou

13) 肝臓 (liver)
kanzou

14) 小腸 (small intestine)
shouchou

15) 大腸 (large intestine)
daichou

16) 胆のう (gallbladder)
tannou

17) 腎臓 (kidney)
jinzou

18) 膀胱 (urinary bladder)
boukou

腎臓の手術をしました。 *Jinzou no shujutsu wo shimashita.*
I had an operation on my kidneys.

たばこは、肺に悪いです。 *Tabako wa hai ni warui desu.*
Smoking is bad for the lungs.

筋肉痛になりました。 *Kinnikutsuu ni narimashita.*
I have sore muscles.

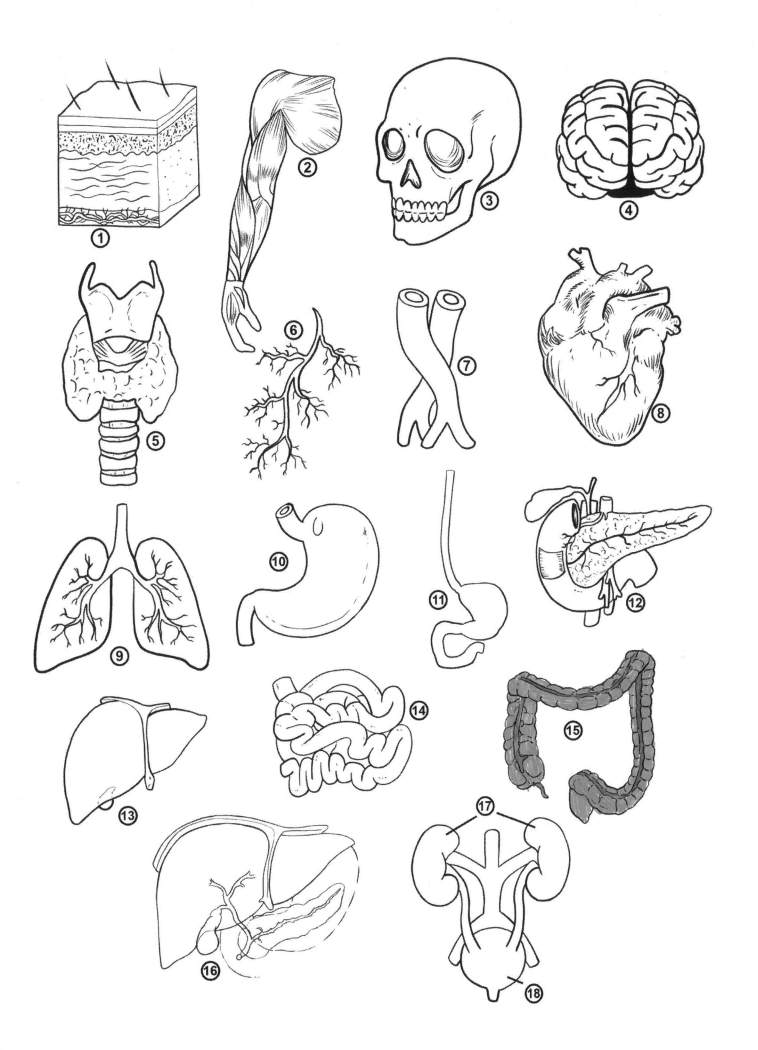

ペット (PETS)

1) 犬 (dog)
いぬ
inu

2) 猫 (cat)
ねこ
neko

3) フェレット (ferret)
feretto

4) ミニブタ (mini pig/teacup pig)
mini buta

5) 馬 (horse)
うま
uma

6) エンゼルフィッシュ (angelfish)
enzeru fisshu

7) クマノミ (clown fish)
kumanomi

8) 金魚 (goldfish)
きんぎょ
kingyo

9) ハムスター (hamster)
hamusutaa

10) モルモット (guinea pig)
morumotto

11) ねずみ (mouse)
nezumi

12) うさぎ (rabbit)
usagi

13) ハリネズミ (hedgehog)
harinezumi

14) タランチュラ (tarantula)
taranchura

15) ありの巣 (ant colony)
す
ari no su

16) 亀 (tortoise)
かめ
kame

17) 蛇 (snake)
へび
hebi

18) カメレオン (chameleon)
kamereon

19) イグアナ (iguana)
iguana

20) カナリア (canary)
kanaria

21) オウム (parrot)
oumu

22) インコ (parakeet)
inko

私 は猫 より犬 のほうが好きです。 *Watashi wa neko yori inu no houga sukidesu.*
わたし ねこ いぬ す
I prefer dogs over cats.

娘 に金魚をプレゼントしました。 *Musume ni kingyo wo purezento shimashita.*
むすめ きんぎょ
I gifted a goldfish to my daughter.

うさぎと亀の競 争の話 をよみました。 *Usagi to kame no kyousou no hanashi wo*
かめ きょうそう はなし
yomimashita.
I read the story of race between the rabbit and tortoise.

32

動物園 (THE ZOO)

1) ゾウ (elephant)
zou

2) サイ (rhino)
sai

3) キリン (giraffe)
kirin

4) シマウマ (zebra)
shimauma

5) カバ (hippopotamus)
kaba

6) チーター (cheetah)
chiitaa

7) トラ (tiger)
tora

8) ライオン (lion)
raion

9) チンパンジー (chimpanzee)
chinpanjii

10) オランウータン (orangutan)
oranuutan

11) ヒヒ (baboon)
hihi

12) カンガルー (kangaroo)
kangaruu

13) コアラ (koala)
koara

14) キツネザル (lemur)
kitsunezaru

ライオンは 百 獣 の王です。 *Raion wa hyakujuu no ou desu.*
The lion is the king of animals.

オーストラリアでコアラを抱きました。 *Oosutoraria de koara wo dakimashita.*
I hugged a koala in Australia.

ゾウはとても 頭 がいいです。 *Zou wa totemo atama ga iidesu.*
Elephants are very intelligent.

34

とり 鳥 (BIRDS)

1) ダチョウ (ostrich)
   dachou

2) クジャク (peacock)
   kujaku

3) シチメンチョウ (turkey)
   shichimenchou

4) ニワトリ (rooster)
   niwatori

5) アヒル (duck)
   ahiru

6) ハクチョウ (swan)
   hakuchou

7) ペリカン (pelican)
   perikan

8) フラミンゴ (flamingo)
   furamingo

9) ハト (pigeon)
   hato

10) フクロウ (owl)
    fukurou

11) ハゲワシ (vulture)
    hagewashi

12) ワシ (eagle)
    washi

13) カモメ (seagull)
    kamome

14) カラス (crow)
    karasu

15) オオハシ (toucan)
    oohashi

16) ペンギン (penguin)
    pengin

17) キツツキ (woodpecker)
    kitsutsuki

18) コンゴウインコ (macaw)
    kongouinko

19) ハチドリ (hummingbird)
    hachidori

20) キーウィ (kiwi)
    kiiwi

ダチョウは世界で一番大きな鳥です。 *Dachou wa sekai de ichiban ookina tori desu.*
The ostrich is the largest bird in the world.

キーウィはニュージーランドの国のシンボルです。 *Kiiwi wa nyuujiirando no kuni no shinboru desu.*
The kiwi is a national symbol of New Zealand.

パラグアイにはハチドリがたくさんいます。 *Paraguai niwa hachidori ga takusan imasu.*
There are many hummingbirds in Paraguay.

QUIZ #1

Use arrows to match the corresponding translations:

a. goldfish

b. leg

c. brother

d. serious

e. flamingo

f. mouse

g. cheetah

h. neighbor

i. cat

j. sad

k. kindness

l. grandson

m. girlfriend

n. curious

o. brain

p. nose

1. <ruby>悲<rt>かな</rt></ruby>しい

2. フラミンゴ

3. <ruby>孫息子<rt>まごむすこ</rt></ruby>

4. <ruby>金魚<rt>きんぎょ</rt></ruby>

5. <ruby>真面目<rt>まじめ</rt></ruby>な

6. チーター

7. <ruby>脚<rt>あし</rt></ruby>

8. <ruby>鼻<rt>はな</rt></ruby>

9. <ruby>兄弟<rt>きょうだい</rt></ruby>

10. <ruby>彼女<rt>かのじょ</rt></ruby>

11. <ruby>気<rt>き</rt></ruby>になる

12. <ruby>脳<rt>のう</rt></ruby>

13. ねずみ

14. <ruby>親切<rt>しんせつ</rt></ruby>

15. <ruby>猫<rt>ねこ</rt></ruby>

16. <ruby>近所<rt>きんじょ</rt></ruby>の<ruby>人<rt>ひと</rt></ruby>

Fill in the blank spaces with the options below (use each word only once):

わたしの＿＿＿＿は２７才です。わたしたちは３年前に、日本で会いました。彼女の
性格はとても＿＿＿＿で、＿＿＿です。＿＿＿が大きくて、＿＿＿＿が短いです。
動物が大好きで、＿＿＿＿を飼っています。昨日は＿＿＿＿をさそって、みんなで
動物園に行きました。＿＿＿＿はとても大きいので、人気があります。彼女の
は３０才で、今ニューヨークに住んでいます。彼女の＿＿＿＿は６０才で、シカゴに住
んでいます。

目 （め）   兄弟 （きょうだい）

ゾウ   お父さん （とう）

彼女 （かのじょ）   親切 （しんせつ）

真面目 （まじめ）   髪 （かみ）

友達 （ともだち）   猫 （ねこ）

爬虫類と両生類 (REPTILES AND AMPHIBIANS)

- 爬虫類 (Reptiles)
  hachuurui

1) アナコンダ (anaconda)
   anakonda

2) キングコブラ (king cobra)
   kingu kobura

3) ガラガラヘビ (rattlesnake)
   garagara hebi

4) サンゴヘビ (coral snake)
   sango hebi

5) ツノトカゲ (horned lizard)
   tsuno tokage

6) エリマキトカゲ (frill-necked lizard)
   erimaki tokage

7) チャイロバシリスク (common basilisk/Jesus Christ lizard)
   chairo bashirisuku

8) コモドドラゴン (Komodo dragon)
   komodo doragon

9) クロコダイル (crocodile)
   kurokodairu

10) インドガビアル (gharial/gavial)
    indo gabiaru

11) ウミガメ (sea turtle)
    umi game

- 両生類 (Amphibians)
  ryouseirui

12) サンショウウオ (salamander)
    sanshouuo

13) ゴライアスガエル (Goliath frog)
    goraiasu gaeru

この川にはクロコダイルがたくさんいます。 *Kono kawa niwa kurokodairu ga takusan imasu.*
This river is full of crocodiles.

ウミガメと一緒に泳ぎたい。 *Umigame to isshoni oyobitai.*
I want to swim with a sea turtle.

キングコブラには毒があります。 *Kingu kobura niwa doku ga arimasu.*
King cobras are venomous.

昆 虫 とクモ類 (INSECTS AND ARACHNIDS)

- 昆 虫 (Insects)
  konchuu

1) ハチ (bee)
   hachi

2) ミツバチ (bumblebee)
   mitsubachi

3) カリバチ (wasp)
   karibachi

4) カブトムシ (beetle)
   kabutomushi

5) チョウ (butterfly)
   chou

6) ガ (moth)
   ga

7) トンボ (dragonfly)
   tonbo

8) テントウムシ (ladybug)
   tentoumushi

9) ホタル (firefly)
   hotaru

10) ゴキブリ (cockroach)
    gokiburi

11) アブ (horsefly)
    abu

12) ハエ (fly)
    hae

13) 蚊 (mosquito)
    ka

14) バッタ (grasshopper)
    batta

15) コオロギ (cricket)
    koorogi

- クモ類 (Arachnids)
  kumo rui

16) サソリ (scorpion)
    sasori

17) クモ (spider)
    kumo

18) クロゴケグモ (Southern black widow)
    kurogoke gumo

クモは嫌いです。 *Kumo wa kirai desu.*
I hate spiders.

ハチに刺されました。 *Hachi ni sasaremashita.*
I got stung by a bee.

毛虫はチョウに変わります。 *Kemushi wa chou ni kawarimasu.*
A caterpillar turns into a butterfly.

哺乳類 I (MAMMALS I)
ほにゅうるい

1) コウモリ (bat)
   koumori

2) カモノハシ (platypus)
   kamonohashi

3) シャチ (killer whale/orca)
   shachi

4) イルカ (dolphin)
   iruka

5) ビーバー (beaver)
   biibaa

6) マーモット (groundhog)
   maamotto

7) モグラ (mole)
   mogura

8) リス (squirrel)
   risu

9) イタチ (weasel)
   itachi

10) オポッサム (possum/opossum)
    opossamu

11) ネズミ (rat)
    nezumi

12) ノウサギ (hare)
    nousagi

13) アナグマ (badger)
    anaguma

14) スカンク (skunk)
    sukanku

15) ヒョウ (leopard)
    hyoo

吸血鬼はコウモリに変わります。 *Kyuuketsuki wa koumori ni kawarimasu.*
きゅうけつき　　　　　　　　か
Vampires turn into bats.

木の上に赤いリスがいます。 *Ki no ue ni akai risu gai masu.*
き　うえ　あか
There is a red squirrel in the tree.

見て、彼女の肩にネズミがのっているよ！ *Mite, Kanojo no kata ni nezumi ga notteiru yo!*
み　　かのじょ　かた
Look, she has a rat on her shoulder!

哺乳類 II (MAMMALS II)

ほにゅうるい

1) クマ (bear)
   kuma

2) ハイエナ (hyena)
   haiena

3) ジャッカル (jackal)
   jakkaru

4) 雌牛 (cow)
   めうし
   meushi

5) 雄牛 (bull)
   おうし
   oushi

6) キツネ (fox)
   kitsune

7) バッファロー (buffalo)
   baffaroo

8) ヘラジカ (elk/moose)
   herajika

9) 羊 (sheep)
   ひつじ
   hitsuji

10) ヤギ (goat)
    yagi

11) ガゼル (gazelle)
    gazeru

12) オオカミ (wolf)
    ookami

13) サル (monkey)
    saru

14) 雄羊 (ram)
    おひつじ
    ohitsuji

15) ロバ (donkey)
    roba

羊の皮を着たオオカミに気をつけろ。 *Hitsuji no kawa wo mita ookami ni kiwotsukero.*
Be aware of the wolf in sheep's clothing.

イエスはロバに乗り、エルサレムに入りました。 *Iesu wa roba ni nori, erusaremu ni hairimashita.*
Jesus rode on the donkey and entered into Jerusalem.

彼はハイエナのように笑った。 *Kare wa haiena no youni waratta.*
He laughed like a hyena.

魚 と 軟 体 動 物 (FISH AND MOLLUSKS)
さかな　　なんたいどうぶつ

- 魚 (Fish)
さかな

  sakana

1) ジンベイザメ (whale shark)
   jinbei zame

2) ホホジロザメ (white shark)
   hohojiro zame

3) シュモクザメ (hammerhead shark)
   shumoku zame

4) メカジキ (swordfish/marlin)
   mekajiki

5) オニカマス (barracuda)
   onikamasu

6) フグ (pufferfish)
   fugu

7) ナマズ (catfish)
   namazu

8) ピラニア (piranha)
   pirania

9) トビウオ (flying fish)
   tobiuo

10) ウツボ (moray eel)
    utsubo

11) マンタ (manta ray)
    manta

12) タツノオトシゴ (seahorse)
    tatsuno otoshigo

- 軟 体 動 物 (Mollusks)
なんたいどうぶつ

  nantai doubutsu

13) イカ (squid)
    ika

14) コウイカ (cuttlefish)
    kouika

15) タコ (octopus)
    tako

16) カキ (oyster)
    kaki

17) アサリ (clam)
    asari

18) オウムガイ (nautilus)
    oumugai

19) カタツムリ (snail)
    katatsumuri

20) ナメクジ (slug)
    namekuji

ホホジロザメに気をつけてください。 *Hohojiro zame ni ki wo tsukete kudasai.*
き
Beware of the white sharks.

日本人は生のカキを食べます。 *Nihonjin wa nama no kaki wo tabemasu.*
にほんじん　なま　　　　た
Japanese eats raw oysters.

私 の父は大きなナマズを捕まえました。 *Watashi no chichi wa ookina namazu wo*
わたし　ちち　おお　　　　　　　つか
tsukamaemashita.
My father caught a huge catfish.

衣服 I (CLOTHING I)

1) レインコート (raincoat)
rein kooto

2) パーカー (hoodie)
paakaa

3) ジャケット (jacket)
jaketto

4) ジーンズ (jeans)
jiinzu

5) ボクサー・ショーツ (boxer shorts)
bokusaa shootsu

6) ブーツ (boots)
buutsu

7) イヤリング (earrings)
iyaringu

8) セーター (sweater)
seetaa

9) ネックレス (necklace)
nekkuresu

10) ブラジャー (bra)
burajaa

11) レギンス (leggings)
reginsu

12) 靴下 (socks)
kutsushita

13) ブラウス / トップス (blouse/top)
burausu / toppusu

14) ブレスレット (bracelet)
buresuretto

15) ショートパンツ (shorts)
shooto pantsu

16) パンティー (panties)
pantii

17) コート (coat)
kooto

18) ワンピース (dress)
wanpiisu

19) ハンドバッグ (purse)
handobaggu

20) サンダル (sandals)
sandaru

レインコートを忘れないで！ *Rein kooto wo wasurenaide !*
Do not forget your raincoat!

私の靴下に穴があいています。 *Watashi no kutsushita ni ana ga aiteimasu.*
There is a hole in my sock.

寒ければ、セーターを着てください。 *Samukereba, seetaa wo kite kudasai.*
If you are cold, wear a sweater.

衣服 II (CLOTHING II)

1) 帽子 (hat)
   boushi

2) タキシード (tuxedo/smoking)
   takishiido

3) ちょうネクタイ (bow tie)
   chou nekutai

4) 靴 (shoes)
   kutsu

5) スーツ (suit)
   suutu

6) シャツ (shirt)
   shatsu

7) ネクタイ (tie)
   nekutai

8) ブリーフケース (briefcase/case)
   buriifu keesu

9) ブラウス (blouse)
   burausu

10) スポーツブラ (sports bra)
    supootsu bura

11) ズボン / パンツ (trousers/pants)
    zubon / pantsu

12) ベルト (belt)
    beruto

13) 指輪 (ring)
    yubiwa

14) T シャツ (T-shirt)
    T shatsu

15) スカート (skirt)
    sukaato

16) マフラー (scarf)
    mafuraa

17) 腕時計 (watch)
    udedokei

18) カーゴパンツ (cargo pants)
    kaago pantsu

19) 財布 (wallet)
    saifu

20) 傘 (umbrella)
    kasa

ブリーフケースの中にお金があります。 *Buriifu keesu no naka ni okane ga arimasu.*
The money is in the briefcase.

日が出ているから、帽子をかぶったほうがいいですよ。 *Hi ga deteiru kara, boushi wo kabutta hou ga iidesuyo.*
The sun is shining, you must wear a hat.

腕時計をなくしました。 *Udedokei wo nakushimashita.*
I have lost my watch.

天気 (THE WEATHER)

1) 晴れ (sunny)
   hare

2) 暑い (hot)
   atsui

3) 砂嵐 (sandstorm)
   suna arashi

4) 曇り (cloudy)
   kumori

5) 暖かい (warm)
   atatakai

6) 霧 (foggy/misty)
   kiri

7) 雨 (rainy)
   ame

8) 涼しい (cool)
   suzushii

9) 雨粒 (raindrop)
   amatsubu

10) むしむしした (humid)
    mushimushi shita

11) 嵐 (storm)
    arashi

12) 雷 (lightning)
    kaminari

13) 風 (windy)
    kaze

14) 雪 (snowy)
    yuki

15) 寒い (cold)
    samui

16) 雪の結晶 (snowflake)
    yuki no kesshou

パラグアイはとても暑い。 *Paraguai wa totemo atsui.*
It is very hot in Paraguay.

晴れているけど寒いです。 *Hareteiru kedo samui desu.*
It is sunny but cold.

東京の夏はとてもむしむしする。 *Tokyo no natsu wa totemo mushimushi suru.*
Summer in Tokyo is very humid.

季節 – 春 (THE SEASONS – SPRING)

1) 庭 (garden)
   niwa

2) 咲く (to bloom)
   saku

3) ピクニック (picnic)
   pikunikku

4) 公園 (park)
   kouen

5) サイクリング (cycling)
   saikuringu

6) レモネード (lemonade)
   remoneedo

7) ガレージ・セール (garage sale)
   gareeji seeru

8) 車の旅 (road trip)
   kuruma no tabi

9) 石で遊ぶ (to paint rocks)
   ishi de asobu

10) 花を植える (to plant some flowers)
    hana wo ueru

11) たこを揚げる (to fly a kite)
    tako wo ageru

12) バーベキューをする (to do a barbecue)
    baabekyuu wo suru

土曜日に私たちは公園でピクニックをします。*Doyoubi ni watashitachi wa kouen de pikunikku wo shimasu.*
On Saturday, we are going to have a picnic in the park.

ロスアンゼルスまで車の旅をします。*Rosuanzerusu made kuruma no tabi wo shimasu.*
I'm going on a road trip to Los Angeles.

暑い日にレモネードを飲むのが好きです。*Atsui hi ni remoneedo wo nomu noga suki desu.*
I like to drink lemonade on a hot day.

季節 – 夏 (THE SEASONS – SUMMER)

1) キャンプに行く (to go camping)
   kyanpu ni iku

2) ウォーターパーク (water park)
   wootaa paaku

3) アウトドア (outdoor activities)
   autodoa

4) プール (swimming pool)
   puuru

5) 泳ぐ (to swim)
   oyogu

6) 日焼けする (to get tanned)
   hiyakesuru

7) 日焼け止め (sunscreen)
   hiyakedome

8) 虫よけ (insect repellent)
   mushiyoke

9) 湖 (lake)
   mizuumi

10) ライフガード (lifesaver/lifeguard)
    raifu gaado

11) 砂の城 (sandcastle)
    suna no shiro

12) ハイキングに行く (to go on a hike)
    haikingu ni iku

湖で泳ぐのが好きです。 *Mizuumi de oyogu noga suki desu.*
I like to swim in a lake.

外に出る前に日焼け止めを塗ってください。 *Soto ni deru maeni hiyakedome wo nutte kudasai.*
Apply sunscreen before you go outside.

私たちはビーチで砂の城を作りました。 *Watashitachi wa biichi de suna no shiro wo tsukurimashita.*
We built a sandcastle on the beach.

QUIZ #2

Use arrows to match the corresponding translations:

a. horsefly

b. mole

c. king cobra

d. coat

e. socks

f. Komodo dragon

g. tie

h. slug

i. ring

j. snail

k. sunny

l. beetle

m. bat

n. warm

o. necklace

p. butterfly

1. モグラ

2. ネクタイ

3. 暖 かい
   <ruby>あたた</ruby>

4. チョウ

5. ネックレス

6. カタツムリ

7. アブ

8. コウモリ

9. キングコブラ

10. ナメクジ

11. カブトムシ

12. 晴れ
    <ruby>は</ruby>

13. コモドドラゴン

14. 指輪
    <ruby>ゆびわ</ruby>

15. 靴 下
    <ruby>くつした</ruby>

16. コート

Fill in the blank spaces with the options below (use each word only once):

サンディは英語の先生です。日曜日に、夫と＿＿＿＿＿＿に行きました。

天気予報は＿＿＿＿＿だったので＿＿＿＿＿を持っていきました。

朝は晴れていて、＿＿＿＿＿＿＿一日でした。日差しが強かったので、

＿をかぶり＿＿＿＿＿を塗りました。山の中で＿＿＿＿をみつけました。

きれいな＿＿＿＿＿もたくさん飛んでいました。

でも、＿＿＿＿も多くて、＿＿＿＿＿を持ってくればよかったと思いました。

ハイキング　　　　　　　　　チョウ

雨　　　　　　　　　　　　　リス

レインコート　　　　　　　　暖かい

帽子　　　　　　　　　　　　日焼け止め

蚊　　　　　　　　　　　　　虫よけ

季節 – 秋 (THE SEASONS – FALL/AUTUMN)

1) 紅葉 (changing leaves)
kouyou

2) 落ち葉を集める (to collect leaves)
ochiba wo atsumeru

3) かぼちゃ (pumpkin)
kabocha

4) かぼちゃを彫る (to carve a pumpkin)
kabocha wo horu

5) りんご狩り (apple picking)
ringo gari

6) ハロウィンの仮装 (Halloween costume)
harowin no kasou

7) ハロウィンキャンディ (Halloween candy)
harowin kyandi

8) アロマキャンドル (scented candles)
aroma kyandoru

9) 感謝祭ディナー (Thanksgiving dinner)
kanshasai dinaa

10) ウールの毛布 (wool blanket)
uuru no moufu

11) マシュマロを焼く (to roast marshmallows)
mashumaro wo yaku

12) 庭を飾る (to decorate the yard)
niwa wo kazaru

ハロウィンのためにかぼちゃを彫りました。*Harowin no tameni kabocha wo horimashita.*
I carved a pumpkin for Halloween.

りんご狩りに行きたいです。*Ringo gari ni ikitaidesu.*
I want to go apple picking.

日本の美しい紅葉は有名です。*Nihon no utsukushii kouyou wa yuumei desu.*
Japan is famous for its beautiful colored leaves.

季節 – 冬 (THE SEASONS – WINTER)

1) ココア (hot cocoa/hot chocolate)
kokoa

2) そり (sled)
sori

3) ミトン (mittens)
miton

4) ダウンジャケット (puffy jacket)
daun jaketto

5) スープ (soup)
suupu

6) ジンジャーブレッドクッキー
(gingerbread cookies)
jinjaa bureddo kukkii

7) 霜の降りた窓 (frosty window)
shimo no orita mado

8) 松ぼっくり (pinecone)
matsubokkuri

9) アイススケート (ice skating)
aisu sukeeto

10) スキー (ski)
sukii

11) スケートリンク (ice rink)
sukeeto rinku

12) 雪玉 (snowball)
yukidama

たき火の近くでココアを飲むのが大好きです。*Takibi no chikaku de kokoa wo nomu noga daisuki desu.*

I love to drink hot chocolate near the fire.

4才の時にスキーを始めました。*Yon sai no toki ni sukii wo hajimemashita.*
I started skiing at the age of 4.

スープができました。*Suupu ga dekimashita.*
The soup is ready.

時間 (TIME)

じかん

1) 時間帯 (time zone)
じかんたい
jikantai

2) 秒 (second)
びょう
byou

3) 分 (minute)
ぶん
fun

4) 時 / 時間 (hour)
じ じかん
ji / jikan

5) 日 / 日 (day)
ひ にち
hi / nichi

6) 週 (week)
しゅう
shuu

7) 二週間 (fortnight)
にしゅうかん
ni shuukan

8) 月 / 月 (month)
つき がつ
tsuki / gatsu

9) 年 (year)
ねん
nen

10) 夜明け (dawn)
よあ
yoake

11) 朝 (morning)
あさ
asa

12) 正午 (noon/midday)
しょうご
shougo

13) 午後 (afternoon)
ごご
gogo

14) 夕方 (dusk)
ゆうがた
yuugata

15) 夜 (night)
よる
yoru

16) 夜中 (midnight)
よなか
yonaka

17) 日付 (date)
ひづけ
hizuke

18) カレンダー (calendar)
karendaa

わたし　むすめ　　　　よる　お
私の娘はよく夜に起きます。 *Watashi no musume wa yoku yoru ni okimasu.*
My daughter wakes up often at night.

きょう　　なんにち
今日は何日ですか。 *Kyou wa nan nichi desuka.*
What day of the month is it today?

わたし　　　　にねんまえ　にほん　い
私たちは二年前に日本に行きました。 *Watashitachi wa ninenmae ni nihon ni ikimashita.*
We visited Japan two years ago.

66

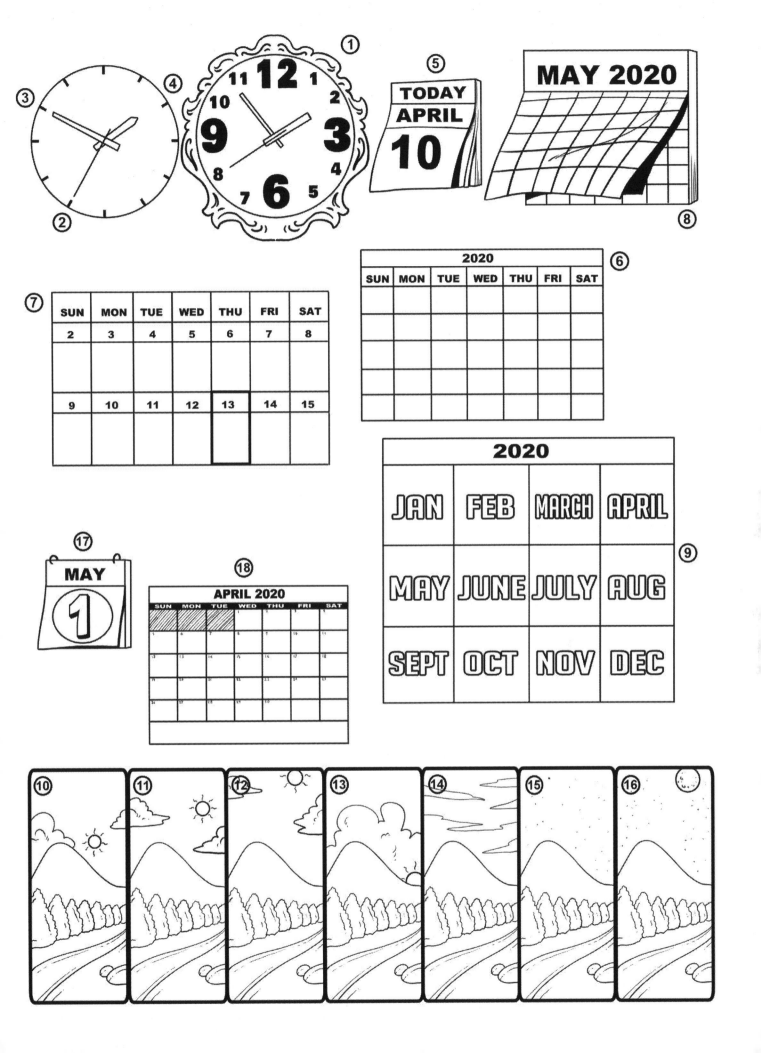

家 (THE HOUSE)

1) 屋根裏 (attic)
   yaneura

2) 屋根 (roof)
   yane

3) 天井 (ceiling)
   tenjou

4) 煙突 (chimney)
   entotsu

5) 壁 (wall)
   kabe

6) バルコニー (balcony)
   barukonii

7) ポーチ (porch)
   poochi

8) 窓 (window)
   mado

9) 雨戸 (shutters)
   amado

10) ドア (door)
    doa

11) 階段 (stairs)
    kaidan

12) 手すり (banister)
    tesuri

13) 床 (floor)
    yuka

14) 地下室 (basement)
    chikashitsu

15) 裏庭 (backyard)
    uraniwa

16) ガレージ (garage)
    gareeji

17) 私道 (driveway)
    shidou

18) フェンス (fence/picket fence)
    fensu

19) ポスト (mailbox)
    posuto

20) 廊下 (hallway/corridor)
    rouka

天井にくもの巣があります。 *Tenjou ni kumonosu ga arimasu.*
There are cobwebs on the ceiling.

とてもきれいな裏庭ですね。 *Totemo kireina uraniwa desune.*
Your backyard is very beautiful.

階段から落ちてしまいました。 *Kaidan kara ochite shimaimashita.*
I fell down the stairs.

キッチン用品 (KITCHEN ITEMS)

1) コンロ (stove)
   konro

2) 電子レンジ (microwave oven)
   denshi renji

3) オーブントースター (toaster oven)
   oobun toosutaa

4) 電動ミキサー (electric mixer)
   dendou mikisaa

5) ミキサー (blender)
   mikisaa

6) トースター (toaster)
   toosutaa

7) コーヒーメーカー (coffee maker)
   koohiimeekaa

8) れいぞうこ (fridge)
   reizouko

9) パントリー (pantry)
   pantorii

10) 食器棚 (cupboard)
    shokkidana

11) ケーキの焼き型 (cake pan)
    keeki no yakigata

12) フライパン (frying pan)
    furaipan

13) 鍋 (pot)
    nabe

14) クッキーの抜き型 (cookie cutters)
    kukkii no nukigata

15) ボウル (mixing bowl)
    bouru

16) 水切りボール (colander)
    mizukiri booru

17) ざる (strainer)
    zaru

18) めん棒 (rolling pin)
    menbou

19) オーブンミトン (oven mitt)
    oobun miton

20) エプロン (apron)
    epuron

ミキサーを使って、スムージーを作りました。 *Mikisaa wo tsukatte, sumuujii wo tsukurimashita.*
I used a blender to make a smoothie.

冷蔵庫の中に卵が三個あります。 *Reizouko no naka ni tamago ga sanko arimasu.*
There are three eggs in the fridge.

電子レンジでコーヒーを温めてください。 *Denshi renji de koohii wo atatamete kudasai.*
Microwave the coffee until hot.

寝室 (BEDROOM ITEMS)

1) ベッド (bed)
   beddo

2) マットレス (mattress)
   mattoresu

3) 寝具 (bedding/bed linen)
   shingu

4) 枕 (pillow)
   makura

5) シーツ (sheets)
   shiitsu

6) 毛布 (blanket)
   moufu

7) ベッドカバー (spread)
   beddo kabaa

8) 枕カバー (pillowcase)
   makura kabaa

9) ナイトテーブル (nightstand)
   naito teeburu

10) 置き時計 (table clock)
    okidokei

11) テーブルライト (table light)
    teeburu raito

12) クローゼット (closet)
    kuroozetto

13) 揺り椅子 (rocking chair)
    yuriisu

14) ランプ (lamp)
    ranpu

15) 鏡 (mirror)
    kagami

16) ドレッサー (dresser)
    doressaa

17) カーテン (curtain)
    kaaten

18) 揺りかご (cradle/crib)
    yurikago

19) ベッドメリー (crib mobile)
    beddo merii

20) ハンガー (hanger)
    hangaa

ベッドのシーツを替えます。 *Beddo no shiitsu wo kaemasu.*
I am going to change the bedsheets.

カーテンを閉めてください。 *Kaaten wo shimete kudasai.*
Please close the curtains.

このマットレスは私には硬過ぎます。 *Kono mattoresu wa watashi niwa katasugimasu.*
This mattress is too hard for me.

お風呂 (BATHROOM ITEMS)

1) シャワーカーテン (shower curtain)
shawaa kaaten

2) タオル (towel)
taoru

3) タオル掛け (towel rack)
taoru kake

4) ハンドタオル (hand towel)
hando taoru

5) バスタブ (bathtub)
basu tabu

6) シャワー (shower)
shawaa

7) トイレ (toilet/WC)
toire

8) 洗面器 (sink/washbasin)
senmenki

9) 蛇口 (faucet/tap)
jaguchi

10) バスマット (bathmat)
basumatto

11) 薬棚 (medicine cabinet)
kusuri dana

12) 歯磨き粉 (toothpaste)
hamigakiko

13) 歯ブラシ (toothbrush)
ha burashi

14) シャンプー (shampoo)
shanpuu

15) くし (comb)
kushi

16) せっけん (soap)
sekken

17) ひげそりクリーム (shaving foam)
higesori

18) ひげそり (razor/shaver)
higesori

19) トイレットペーパー (toilet paper)
toiretto peepaa

20) ラバーカップ (plunger)
rabaa kappu

21) トイレブラシ (toilet brush)
toire burashi

22) ごみ箱 (wastebasket)
gomibako

トイレットペーパーがもうありません！ *Toiretto peepaa ga mou arimasen !*
There is no more toilet paper!

タオルはタオル掛けにおいてください。 *Taoru wa taoru kake ni oite kudasai.*
Place the towel on the towel rack.

新しい歯ブラシを買わなきゃいけません。 *Atarashii ha burashi wo kawanakya ikemasen.*
I have to buy a new toothbrush.

リビングルーム (LIVING ROOM ITEMS)

1) 家具 (furniture)
かぐ
kagu

2) 椅子 (chair)
いす
isu

3) ソファー (sofa)
sofaa

4) 長椅子 (couch)
ながいす
nagaisu

5) クッション (cushion)
kusshon

6) コーヒーテーブル (coffee table)
koohii teeburu

7) 灰皿 (ashtray)
はいざら
haizara

8) 花瓶 (vase)
かびん
kabin

9) 飾り (ornaments)
かざ
kazari

10) 本棚 (bookshelf/bookcase)
ほんだな
hondana

11) 本立て (magazine holder)
ほんた
hontate

12) ステレオ (stereo)
sutereo

13) スピーカー (speakers)
supiikaa

14) 暖炉 (fireplace)
だんろ
danro

15) シャンデリア (chandelier)
shanderia

16) ランプ (lamp)
ranpu

17) 電球 (light bulb)
でんきゅう
denkyuu

18) 掛け時計 (wall clock)
か　どけい
kakedokei

19) 絵 (painting)
え
e

20) テレビ (TV/television)
terebi

21) リモコン (remote control)
rimokon

22) ゲーム機 (video game console)
き
geemuki

テレビを見過ぎた。 *Terebi wo misugita.*
みす
I spent too much time watching TV.

クリスマスには夫にゲーム機を買いました。 *Kurisumasu niwa otto ni geemuki wo kaimashita.*
おっと　　　き　か
I bought my husband a video game console for Christmas.

妻はソファーで寝ています。 *Tsuma wa sofaa de neteimasu.* My wife is sleeping on the sofa.
つま　　　　　　ね

ダイニングルーム (DINING ROOM ITEMS)

1) ダイニングテーブル(dining table)
dainingu teeburu

2) テーブルクロス (tablecloth)
teeburu kurosu

3) テーブルセンター (centerpiece)
teeburu sentaa

4) ランチョンマット (placemat)
ranchon matto

5) お皿 (plate)
osara

6) ナプキン (napkin)
napukin

7) ナイフ (knife)
naifu

8) フォーク (fork)
fooku

9) スプーン (spoon)
supuun

10) 水差し (pitcher/jar)
mizusashi

11) コップ (glass)
koppu

12) マグカップ (mug/cup)
magukappu

13) 塩入れ (salt shaker)
shioire

14) コショウ入れ (pepper shaker)
koshouire

15) トレイ (tray)
torei

16) 飲み物 (drink/beverage)
nomimono

17) 食べ物 (food)
tabemono

18) おやつ (snack)
oyatsu

トレイにのせて朝ごはんを持っていきます。 *Torei ni nosete asagohan wo motte ikimasu.*
I will bring you breakfast on a tray.

飲み物はいかがですか？ *Nomimono wa ikaga desuka ?*
Would you like something to drink?

私は日本の食べ物が大好きです。 *Watashi wa nihon no tabemono ga daisuki desu.*
I love Japanese food.

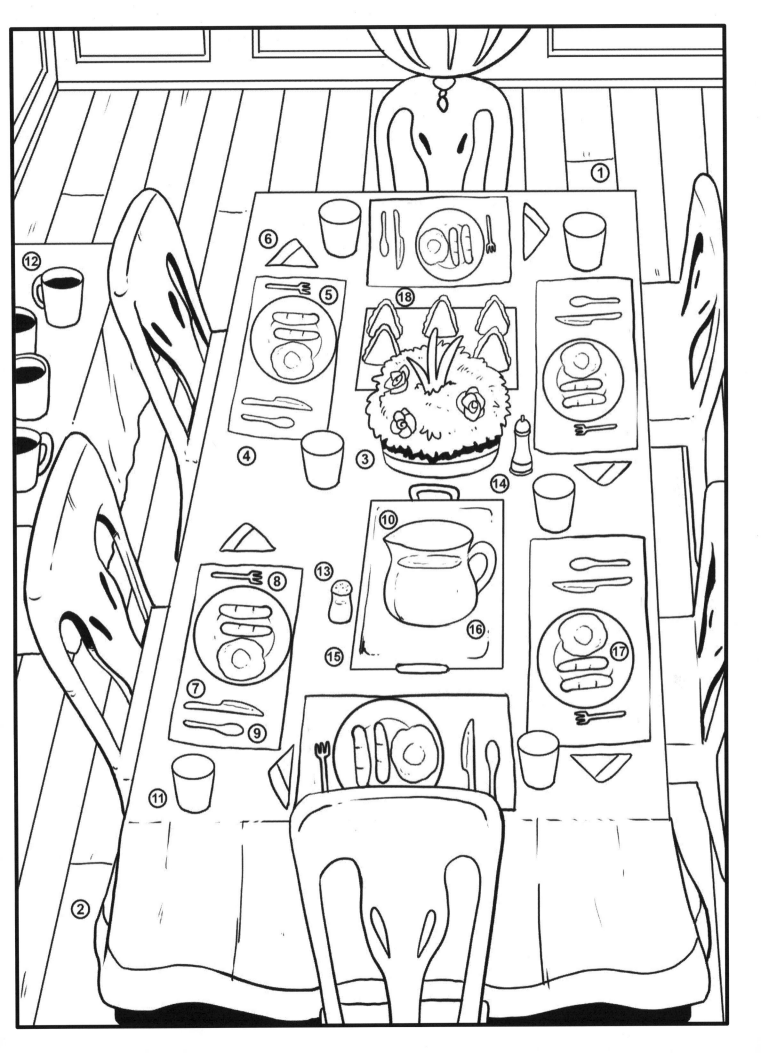

QUIZ #3

Use arrows to match the corresponding translations:

a. morning

b. pumpkin

c. door

d. Halloween costume

e. pillow

f. afternoon

g. sled

h. apron

i. ice rink

j. towel rack

k. wall

l. closet

m. window

n. fireplace

o. snowball

p. toaster

1. ドア

2. <ruby>朝<rt>あさ</rt></ruby>

3. かぼちゃ

4. エプロン

5. <ruby>壁<rt>かべ</rt></ruby>

6. クローゼット

7. <ruby>暖炉<rt>だんろ</rt></ruby>

8. ハロウィンコスチューム

9. <ruby>枕<rt>まくら</rt></ruby>

10. <ruby>雪玉<rt>ゆきだま</rt></ruby>

11. そり

12. スケートリンク

13. <ruby>午後<rt>ごご</rt></ruby>

14. トースター

15. タオル<ruby>掛<rt>か</rt></ruby>け

16. <ruby>窓<rt>まど</rt></ruby>

Fill in the blank spaces with the options below (use each word only once):

これが 私 の家 です。最近＿＿＿＿を黄色に塗りました。＿＿＿＿には大 きな木があり

ます。秋 になると＿＿＿＿がとてもきれいです。でも、＿＿＿＿のはたいへんです。

冬 の寒 い日 には、＿＿＿＿で＿＿＿＿を飲 むのが好 きです。雪 が降 れば、 弟 と

を作 って遊 びます。リビングルームの＿＿＿＿に火 をつけて、＿＿＿＿で本 を読 むのも

大好 きです。日曜日 はみんなで＿＿＿＿を見 ます。

テレビ

裏庭

ソファー

落ち葉を集 める

壁

雪玉

ココア

暖炉

バルコニー

紅葉

にわ
庭 (THE GARDEN/THE BACKYARD)

1) 庭師 (gardener)
   niwashi

2) 倉庫 (shed)
   souko

3) 茂み (bush)
   shigemi

4) 芝生 (lawn)
   shibafu

5) 草 (grass)
   kusa

6) 花 (flower)
   hana

7) ホース (garden hose)
   hoosu

8) じょうろ (watering can)
   jouro

9) 植木 (flowerpot)
   ueki

10) ガーデニング手袋 (gardening gloves)
    gaadeningu tebukuro

11) シャベル (shovel)
    shaberu

12) 熊手 (rake)
    kumade

13) ガーデンフォーク (gardening fork)
    gaaden fooku

14) せん定ばさみ (pruners/pruning shears)
    senteibasami

15) スコップ (garden trowel)
    sucoppu

16) 蛇口 (tap)
    jaguchi

17) 手押し車 (wheelbarrow)
    teoshi guruma

18) 芝刈り機 (lawn mower)
    shibakariki

19) ランタン (lantern)
    rantan

20) つる (vine)
    tsuru

一週間に一度芝生を刈ります。 *Isshuukan ni ichido shibafu wo karimasu.*
I mow the lawn once a week.

倉庫を整理しなきゃいけません。 *Souko wo seiri shinakya ikemasen.*
I have to organize the shed.

私たちは花が咲くのを待っています。 *Watashitachi wa hana ga saku nowo matteimasu.*
We are waiting for the flowers to bloom.

ランドリールーム (THE CLEANING ROOM)

1) 洗濯機 (washing machine)
せんたくき
sentakuki

2) 乾燥機 (dryer)
かんそうき
kansouki

3) アイロン (iron)
airon

4) アイロン台 (ironing board)
だい
airon dai

5) 洗濯せっけん (laundry soap)
せんたく
sentaku sekken

6) 合成洗剤 (laundry detergent)
ごうせいせんざい
gousei senzai

7) 柔軟剤 (fabric softener)
じゅうなんざい
juunanzai

8) 洗濯かご (laundry basket)
せんたく
sentaku kago

9) 汚れた服 (dirty clothes)
よご　ふく
yogoreta fuku

10) 洗濯済みの服 (clean laundry)
せんたくず　　ふく
sentakuzumi no fuku

11) ほうき (broom)
houki

12) ちりとり (dust pan)
chiritori

13) ゴム手袋 (rubber gloves)
てぶくろ
gomu tebukuro

14) スポンジ (sponge)
suponji

15) たらい (plastic tub)
tarai

16) モップ (mop)
moppu

17) バケツ (bucket)
baketsu

18) ぞうきん (cleaning cloths)
zoukin

19) ブラシ (scrub brush)
burashi

20) 漂白剤 (bleach)
ひょうはくざい
hyouhakuzai

21) 消毒剤 (disinfectant)
しょうどくざい
shoudokuzai

22) ごみ箱 (garbage can)
ばこ
gomibako

洗濯するのは嫌いです。 *Sentakusuru nowa kirai desu.*
せんたく　　　　きら
I don't like doing the laundry.

床をモップがけしてください。 *Yuka wo moppu gake shite kudasai.*
ゆか
You must mop the floor.

洗濯機に柔軟剤を入れても大丈夫です。 *Sentakuki ni juunanzai wo iretemo daijoubudesu.*
せんたくき　じゅうなんざい　い　　　　だいじょうぶ
You can use fabric softener in the washing machine.

学校 / 大学 (THE SCHOOL/THE UNIVERSITY)

1) 先生 (teacher)
sensei

2) 学生 (student)
gakusei

3) 教室 (classroom)
kyoushitsu

4) ロッカー (locker)
rokkaa

5) 掲示板 (bulletin board)
keiji ban

6) 紙 (sheet of paper)
kami

7) 本 (book)
hon

8) ノート (notebook)
nooto

9) のり (glue)
nori

10) はさみ (scissors)
hasami

11) えんぴつ (pencil)
enpitsu

12) 消しゴム (eraser)
keshigomu

13) えつぴつ削り (pencil sharpener)
enpitsu kezuri

14) ペン (pen)
pen

15) マーカー (marker)
maakaa

16) 蛍光ペン (highlighter)
keikou pen

17) 封筒 (envelope)
fuutou

18) クリップボード (clipboard)
kurippu boodo

19) 黒板 (blackboard)
kokuban

20) 電卓 (calculator)
dentaku

21) 定規 (ruler)
jougi

22) ホッチキス (stapler)
hocchikisu

23) 筆箱 (pouch/pencil case)
fudebako

24) 机 (school desk)
tsukue

25) 教壇 (table)
kyoudan

26) ノートパソコン (laptop)
nooto pasokon

電卓なしでこの計算をするのはたいへんです。 *Dentaku nashi de kono keisan wo suru nowa taihen desu.* This calculation is complicated without a calculator.

間違いをなおすのに消しゴムを使ってください。 *Machigai wo naosu noni keshigomu wo tsukatte kudasai.*

Use your eraser to correct your mistake.

私のえんぴつ削りが見つかりません。 *Watashi no enpitsu kezuri ga mitsukarimasen.*

I cannot find my pencil sharpener.

オフィス (THE OFFICE)

1) 上司 (boss)
じょうし
joushi

2) 先輩 (superior)
せんぱい
senpai

3) 従業員 (employee)
じゅうぎょういん
juugyouin

4) 社長 (CEO/president)
しゃちょう
shachou

5) ビジネスパートナー (business partner)
bijinesu paatonaa

6) 仕事仲間 (colleague)
しごとなかま
shigoto namaka

7) 同僚 (co-worker)
どうりょう
douryou

8) 秘書 (secretary)
ひしょ
hisho

9) 仕事場 (cubicle)
しごとば
shigotoba

10) 回転椅子 (swivel chair)
かいてんいす
kaiten isu

11) 机 / デスク (desk)
つくえ
tsukue / desuku

12) パソコン (computer)
pasokon

13) プリンター (printer)
purintaa

14) 事務用品 (office supplies)
じむようひん
jimu youhin

15) はんこ (rubber stamp)
hanko

16) テープカッター (tape dispenser)
teepu kattaa

17) フォルダー (folder)
forudaa

18) オフィスキャビネット (filing cabinet)
ofisu kyabinetto

19) ファックス (fax)
fakkusu

20) 電話 (telephone)
でんわ
denwa

新しい仕事仲間が大好きです。 *Atarashii shigoto nakama ga daisuki desu.*
あたら　　　しごとなかま　だいす
I really like my new colleague.

秘書は電話が鳴っているのに気づかなかった。 *Hisho wa denwa ga natteiru noni kizukanakatta.*
ひしょ　でんわ　な　　　　　　　　　　き
The secretary didn't notice the phone ringing.

ファックスを使う人なんてもういないよ！ *Fakkusu wo tsukau hito nante mou inaiyo !*
つか　ひと
No one uses a fax anymore!

せんもんしょく 専門職 (PROFESSIONS/OCCUPATIONS)

1) エンジニア (engineer)
   enginia

2) うちゅうひこうし 宇宙飛行士 (astronaut)
   uchuu hikoushi

3) パイロット (pilot)
   pairotto

4) さいばんかん 裁判官 (judge)
   saibankan

5) しょうぼうし 消防士 (firefighter)
   shouboushi

6) けいさつかん 警察官 (police officer)
   keisatsukan

7) りょうりにん 料理人 (chef)
   ryourinin

8) しきしゃ 指揮者 (conductor)
   shikisha

9) きょうじゅ 教授 (professor)
   kyouju

10) ダンサー (dancer)
    dansaa

11) ビジネスマン (businessman)
    bijinesuman

12) アニマル・トレーナー (animal trainer)
    animaru toreenaa

こ とき
子どもの時、パイロットになりたかった。 *Kodomo no toki, pairotto ni naritakatta.*
When I was a kid, I wanted to be a pilot.

かれ
彼はいいビジネスマンになるだろうね。 *Kare wa ii bijinesuman ni naru daroune.*
He will become a good businessman.

しょうぼうし よ
消防士を呼んでください！ *Shouboushi wo yonde kudasai!*
Call the firefighters!

交通機関 (MEANS OF TRANSPORT)

こうつうきかん

1) 自転車 (bike/bicycle)
じてんしゃ
jitensha

2) バイク (motorcycle/motorbike)
baiku

3) スノーモービル (snowmobile)
snoomoobiru

4) 車 (car/automobile)
くるま
kuruma

5) バス (bus)
basu

6) トラック (truck)
torakku

7) 地下鉄 (subway)
ちかてつ
chikatetsu

8) 電車 (train)
でんしゃ
densha

9) 水上バイク (jet ski)
すいじょう
suijou baiku

10) 船 (boat)
ふね
fune

11) クルーズ船 (cruise ship)
せん
kuruuzu sen

12) 潜水艦 (submarine)
せんすいかん
sensuikan

13) 飛行船 (blimp/Zeppelin)
ひこうせん
hikousen

14) 気球 (hot-air balloon)
ききゅう
kikyuu

15) 飛行機 (plane/airplane)
ひこうき
hikouki

16) ヘリコプター (helicopter/chopper)
herikoputaa

17) スペースシャトル (space shuttle)
supeesu shatoru

バスで行きますか？それとも車? *Basu de ikimasuka? Soretomo kuruma?*
い　　　　　　　　　　　くるま
Are you going to take the bus or your car?

飛行機に乗るのがこわいです。*Hikouki ni noru noga kowai desu.*
ひこうき　の
I am scared of flying.

電車で京都に行きます。*Densha de Kyoto ni ikimasu.*
でんしゃ　きょうと　い
I am going to Kyoto by train.

92

景色 (LANDSCAPES)

1) 山 (mountain)
yama

2) 熱帯雨林 (tropical rainforest)
nettai urin

3) 砂漠 (desert)
sabaku

4) 火山 (volcano)
kazan

5) 崖 (cliff)
gake

6) ビーチ (beach)
biichi

7) 森 (forest)
mori

8) 洞窟 (cave)
doukutsu

9) 間欠泉 (geyser)
kanketsusen

10) 滝 (waterfall/falls)
taki

11) 川 (river)
kawa

12) 遺跡 (ancient ruins)
iseki

森の中で迷いました。 *Mori no naka de mayoimashita.*
I got lost in the forest.

イグアスの滝は世界で一番大きい滝です。 *Iguasu no taki wa sekai de ichiban ookii taki desu.*
The Iguazu Falls is the biggest waterfall in the world.

この川を渡らなきゃいけません。 *Kono kawa wo wataranakya ikemasen.*
We must cross the river.

スポーツ I (SPORTS I)

1) アーチェリー (archery)
   aacherii

2) ボクシング (boxing)
   bokushingu

3) サイクリング (cycling)
   saikuringu

4) フェンシング (fencing)
   fenshingu

5) サッカー (football/soccer)
   sakkaa

6) ラグビー (rugby)
   ragubii

7) 卓球 (table tennis)
   takkyuu

8) バレー (volleyball)
   varee

9) 重量挙げ (weightlifting)
   juuryouage

10) スケート (skating)
    sukeeto

11) パラリンピック・スポーツ
    (paralympic sports)
    pararinpikku supootsu

12) 野球 (baseball)
    yakyuu

13) バスケットボール / バスケ (basketball)
    basuketto booru / basuke

ラグビー選手は本当にすごいと思います。 *Ragubii senshu wa hontou ni sugoi to omoimasu.*
I really admire rugby players.

重量挙げをしにジムに行きます。 *Juuryouage wo shini jimu ni ikimasu.*
I go to the gym to do weightlifting.

日本人は野球が大好きです。 *Nihonjin wa yakyuu ga daisuki desu.*
Japanese love baseball.

スポーツ II (SPORTS II)

1) バトミントン (badminton)
   batominton

2) 体操 (gymnastics)
   たいそう
   taisou

3) ボート (rowing)
   booto

4) ロッククライミング (rock climbing)
   rokku kuraimingu

5) サーフィン (surfing)
   saafin

6) テニス (tennis)
   tenisu

7) トランポリン (trampoline)
   toranporin

8) レスリング (wrestling)
   resuringu

9) スキー (skiing)
   sukii

10) スケルトン (skeleton)
    sukeruton

11) フィギュアスケート (figure skating)
    figyua sukeeto

12) 水泳 (swimming)
    すいえい
    suiei

13) 水球 (water polo)
    すいきゅう
    suikyuu

14) アイスホッケー (hockey)
    aisu hokkee

スキーは日本でとても人気です。 *Sukii wa nihon de totemo ninki desu.*
Skiing is very popular in Japan.

大阪なおみは最高のテニス選手の一人です。 *Osaka Naomi wa saikou no tenisu senshu no hitori desu.*
Naomi Osaka is one of the best tennis players.

水球のルールは知りません。 *Suikyuu no ruuru wa shirimasen.*
I do not know the rules of water polo.

クリスマス (CHRISTMAS DAY)

1) ヤドリギ (mistletoe)
yadorigi

2) クリスマスリース (garland)
kurisumasu riisu

3) クリスマスツリー (Christmas tree)
kurisumasu tsurii

4) クリスマスの飾り (Christmas decorations)
kurisumasu no kazari

5) クリスマスプレゼント (Christmas gifts)
kurisumasu purezento

6) クリスマスディナー (Christmas dinner)
kurisumasu dinaa

7) キャンディケイン (candy cane)
kyandi kein

8) ジンジャーブレッドマン (gingerbread man)
ginjaa bureddo man

9) クリスマスのエルフ (Christmas elf)
kurisumasu no erufu

10) サンタ帽子 (Christmas hat)
santa no boushi

11) サンタクロース (Santa Claus)
santa kuroosu

12) サンタのそり (Santa's sleigh)
santa no sori

13) クリスマススター (Christmas star)
kurisumasu sutaa

14) 雪だるま (snowman)
yukidaruma

15) ろうそく (candles)
rousoku

私たちはクリスマスディナーでサーモンを食べます。 *Watashitachi wa kurisumasu dinaa de saamon wo tabemasu.*
We will eat salmon for Christmas dinner.

サンタクロースは煙突から入ってきます。 *Santa kuroosu wa entotsu kara haittekimasu.*
Santa Claus enters through the chimney.

わたしはクリスマスツリーを買いませんでした。 *Watashitachi wa kurisumasu tsurii wo kaimasendeshita.*
I didn't buy a Christmas tree.

QUIZ #4

Use arrows to match the corresponding translations:

a. engineer

b. printer

c. wheelbarrow

d. mop

e. colleague

f. gardener

g. bike

h. cave

i. plane

j. calculator

k. firefighter

l. boat

m. dirty clothes

n. washing machine

o. rake

p. classroom

1. 洞窟
どうくつ

2. 船
ふね

3. 自転車
じてんしゃ

4. 汚れた服
よご　　　ふく

5. 庭師
にわし

6. 洗濯機
せんたくき

7. 仕事仲間
しごとなかま

8. 熊手
くまで

9. モップ

10. 消防士
しょうぼうし

11. 手押し車
て お　　ぐるま

12. 教室
きょうしつ

13. プリンター

14. 電卓
でんたく

15. エンジニア

16. 飛行機
ひこうき

Fill in the blank spaces with the options below (use each word only once):

アンドリューは IT＿＿＿＿です。シカゴのオフィスで 働^{はたら}いていて、＿＿＿＿からも 信 頼^{しんらい} されています。＿＿＿＿にくわしく、壊^{こわ}れたらすぐに 直^{なお}してくれます。休 日^{きゅうじつ} は、旅 行^{りょこう} するのが大好^{だいす}きです。＿＿＿＿に乗^のってカリブ 海^{かい}を旅^{たび}したり、＿＿＿＿で日本^{にほん}に行^いったり しました。イタリアのローマで見^みた＿＿＿＿はすばらしいと言っていました。

自然^{しぜん}が大好^{だいす}きで、友 達^{ともだち}と＿＿＿＿に 登^{のぼ}ったり、＿＿＿＿で 泳^{およ}ぐこともあります。スポーツも 得意^{とくい}で、日曜日^{にちようび}は 毎 週^{まいしゅう}＿＿＿＿＿をしています。でも寒^{さむ}いのが苦手^{にがて}で、＿＿＿＿や アイススケートはあまりしません。

エンジニア	遺跡^{いせき}
スキー	飛行機^{ひこうき}
山^{やま}	クルーズ船^{せん}
バスケットボール	パソコン
川^{かわ}	上司^{じょうし}

楽器 (MUSICAL INSTRUMENTS)

がっき

1) アコースティックギター (acoustic guitar)
   akoosutikku gitaa

2) エレキギター (electric guitar)
   ereki gitaa

3) ベースギター (bass guitar)
   beesu gitaa

4) ドラム (drums)
   doramu

5) ピアノ (piano)
   piano

6) トランペット (trumpet)
   tranpetto

7) ハーモニカ (harmonica)
   haamonika

8) フルート (flute)
   furuuto

9) クラリネット (clarinet)
   kurarinetto

10) ハープ (harp)
    haapu

11) バグパイプ (bagpipes)
    bagupaipu

12) チェロ (cello)
    chero

13) バイオリン (violin)
    baiorin

14) サックス (saxophone)
    sakkusu

ピアノのレッスンを始めました。 *Piano no ressun wo hajimemashita.*
I have started taking piano lessons.

ハープは私の好きな楽器です。 *Haapu wa watashi no sukina gakki desu.*
The harp is my favorite instrument.

ジミ・ヘンドリックスはギターの天才だ。 *Jimi Hendorikkusu wa gitaa no tensai da.*
Jimmy Hendrix was a guitar genius.

フルーツ (FRUITS)

1) イチゴ (strawberry)
ichigo

2) パパイヤ (papaya)
papaiya

3) プラム (plum)
puramu

4) メロン (melon)
meron

5) スイカ (watermelon)
suika

6) バナナ (banana)
banana

7) マンゴー (mango)
mangoo

8) モモ (peach)
momo

9) ラズベリー (raspberry)
razuberii

10) オレンジ (orange)
orenji

11) レモン (lemon)
remon

12) パイナップル (pineapple)
painappuru

13) ライム (lime)
raimu

14) ブドウ (grapes)
budou

15) チェリー (cherry)
cherii

16) リンゴ (apple)
ringo

17) ナシ (pear)
nashi

18) グレープフルーツ (grapefruit)
gureepu furuutsu

19) サワーソップ (soursop)
sawaasoppu

20) ココナッツ (coconut)
kokonattsu

ナシを1キロほしいです。 *Nashi wo ichi kiro hoshii desu.*
I would like a kilo of pears.

彼は朝ごはんでバナナを食べます。 *Kare wa asagohan de banana wo tabemasu.*
He eats a banana for breakfast.

イチゴジャムが大好きです。 *Ichigo jamu ga daisuki desu.*
I love strawberry jam.

野菜 (VEGETABLES)

1) カリフラワー (cauliflower)
   karifurawaa

2) アスパラガス (asparagus)
   asuparagasu

3) ブロッコリー (broccoli)
   burokkorii

4) キャベツ (cabbage)
   kyabetsu

5) アーティチョーク (artichoke)
   aatichooku

6) メキャベツ (Brussels sprout)
   mekyabetsu

7) とうもろこし (corn)
   toumorokoshi

8) レタス (lettuce)
   retasu

9) ほうれんそう (spinach)
   hourensou

10) トマト (tomato)
    tomato

11) きゅうり (cucumber)
    kyuuri

12) ズッキーニ (zucchini)
    zukkiini

13) マッシュルーム (mushroom)
    masshuruumu

14) ルッコラ (arugula)
    rukkora

15) なす (eggplant)
    nasu

16) ピーマン (bell pepper)
    piiman

17) たまねぎ (onion)
    tamanegi

18) かぼちゃ (pumpkin/squash)
    kabocha

19) じゃがいも (potato)
    jagaimo

20) スイスチャード (Swiss chard)
    suisuchaado

キャベツスープを用意しました。 *Kyabetsu suupu wo youi shimashita.*
I prepared a cabbage soup.

トマトサラダはソースがありません。 *Tomato sarada wa soosu ga arimasen.*
The tomato salad lacks sauce.

サーモンのグリルとアスパラガスはよく合います。 *Saamon no guriru to asuparagasu wa aimasu.*
Grilled salmon goes well with asparagus.

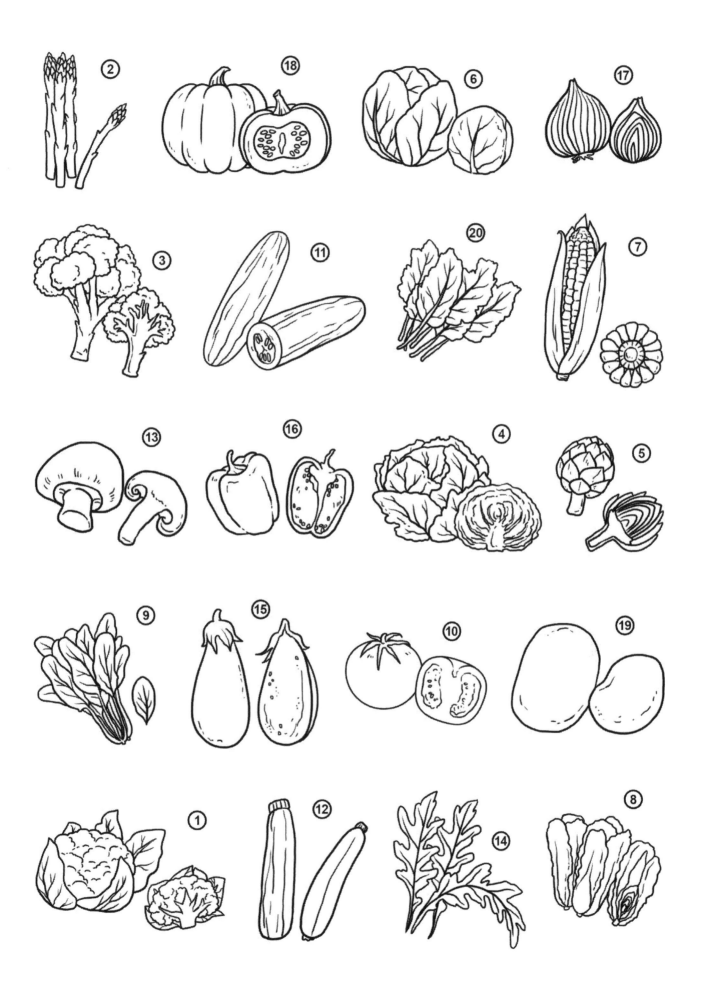

テクノロジー (TECHNOLOGY)

1) 携帯電話 (mobile)
けいたいでんわ
keitai denwa

2) デバイス (device)
debaisu

3) パソコン (computer)
pasokon

4) ウェブカメラ (web cam)
webukamera

5) フラッシュドライブ (flash drive)
furasshu doraibu

6) ハードドライブ (hard drive)
haado doraibu

7) メモリーカード (memory card)
memorii kaado

8) カードリーダー (card reader)
kaado riidaa

9) ワイヤレス (wireless)
waiyaresu

10) ソーラーパネル (solar panel)
sooraa paneru

11) プリンター (printer)
purintaa

12) スキャナー (scanner)
sukyanaa

ウェブカメラを使ってミーティングがあります。 *Webukamera wo tsukatte miitingu ga arimasu.*
I have a meeting via webcam.

カメラのメモリーカードがいっぱいです。 *Kamera no memorii kaado ga ippai desu.*
My camera's memory card is full.

フラッシュドライブにこのドキュメントを保存します。 *Furasshu doraibu ni kono dokyumento wo hozon shimasu.*
I am going to save these documents on my flash drive.

科学 (SCIENCE)
<small>かがく</small>

1) 研究室 (laboratory)
<small>けんきゅうしつ</small>
kenkyuu shitsu

2) 研究者 (researcher)
<small>けんきゅうしゃ</small>
kenkyuu sha

3) 計算 (calculations)
<small>けいさん</small>
keisan

4) 科学者 (scientist)
<small>かがくしゃ</small>
kagakusha

5) 実験用白衣 (lab coat)
<small>じっけんようはくい</small>
jikken you hakui

6) 実験 (experiment)
<small>じっけん</small>
jikken

7) 個人用防護具 (personal protective equipment)
<small>こじんようぼうごぐ</small>
kojin you bougogu

8) 検査 (test)
<small>けんさ</small>
kensa

9) 賞 (prize)
<small>しょう</small>
shou

10) リスク (risk)
risuku

11) 実験器具 (instrument)
<small>じっけんきぐ</small>
jikken kigu

12) 統計値 (statistics)
<small>とうけいち</small>
toukeichi

研究室では実験用白衣を着なきゃいけません。 *Kenkyuu shitsu dewa jikken you hakui wo kinakya ikemasen.*
You must wear a lab coat in the laboratory.

PCR検査を受けに来ました。 *PCR kensa wo ukeni kimashita.*
I have come for a PCR test.

彼は科学者として働いています。 Kare wa kagakusha toshite hataraiteimasu.
He works as a scientist.

てんもんがく
天文学 (ASTRONOMY)

1) ぼうえんきょう
   望遠鏡 (telescope)
   bouenkyou

2) たいよう
   太陽 (sun)
   taiyou

3) つき
   月 (moon)
   tsuki

4) ぎんが
   銀河 (galaxy)
   ginga

5) しょうわくせいたい
   小惑星帯 (asteroid belt)
   shouwakuseitai

6) ブラックホール (black hole)
   burakku hooru

7) にっしょく
   日食 (eclipse)
   nisshoku

8) なが　ぼし
   流れ星 (shooting star)
   nagareboshi

9) うちゅう
   宇宙ステーション (space station)
   uchuu suteeshon

10) はくしょく　せい
    白色わい星 (white dwarf)
    hakushoku waisei

11) せきしょくきょせい
    赤色巨星 (red giant)
    sekishoku kyosei

12) きどう
    軌道 (orbit)
    kidou

13) せいざ
    星座 (constellation)
    seiza

14) ダークエネルギー (dark energy)
    daaku enerugii

15) おうせい
    めい王星 (Pluto)
    meiousei

16) せいうん
    星雲 (Nebula)
    seiun

17) すいせい
    水星 (Mercury)
    suisei

18) きんせい
    金星 (Venus)
    kinsei

19) ちきゅう
    地球 (Earth)
    chikyuu

20) かせい
    火星 (Mars)
    kasei

21) もくせい
    木星 (Jupiter)
    mokusei

22) どせい
    土星 (Saturn)
    dosei

23) てんのうせい
    天王星 (Uranus)
    tennousei

24) かいおうせい
    海王星 (Neptune)
    kaiou sei

うちゅう　　　　　　　かせい　とうちゃく
宇宙ステーションが火星に到着しました。 *Uchuu suteeshon ga kasei ni touchaku shimashita.*
The space station landed on Mars.

つき　ある　　さいしょ　にんげん
ニール・アームストロングは月を歩いた最初の人間です。 *Niiru aamusutorongu wa tsuki wo aruita saisho no ningen desu.*
Neil Armstrong is the first person to walk on the Moon.

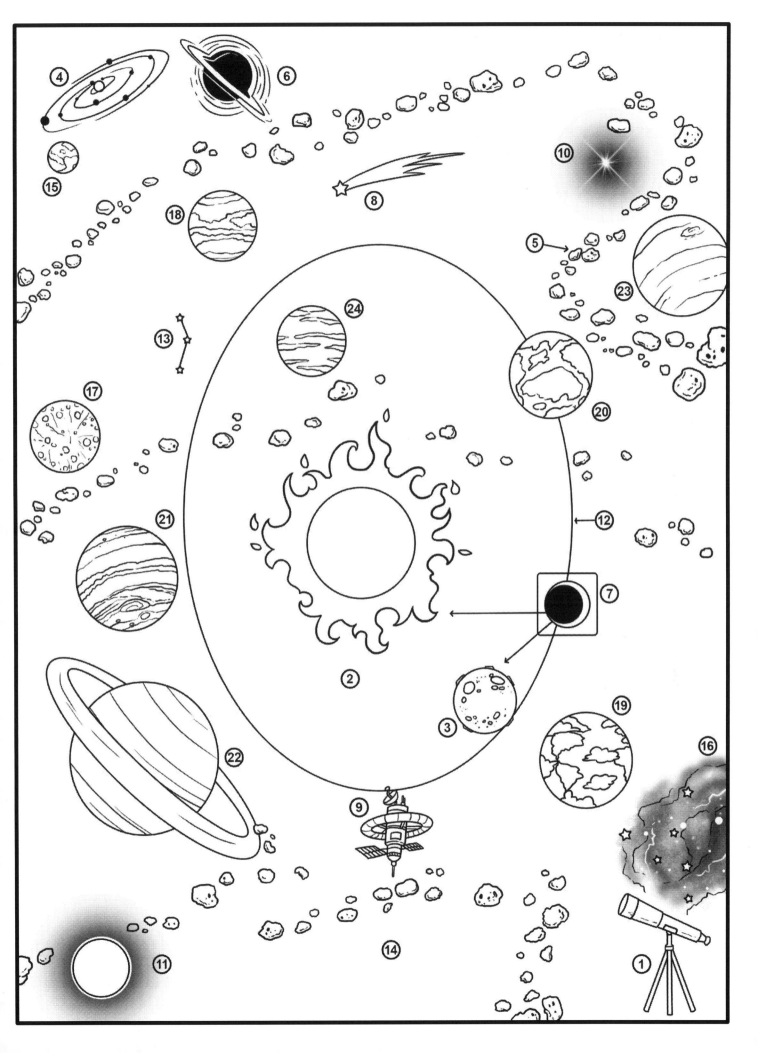

地理 (GEOGRAPHY)
ちり

1) 北 (north)
   きた
   kita

2) 東 (east)
   ひがし
   higashi

3) 南 (south)
   みなみ
   minami

4) 西 (west)
   にし
   nishi

5) 赤 道 (Equator)
   せきどう
   sekidou

6) 北 回 帰 線 (Tropic of Cancer)
   きたかいきせん
   kita kaikisen

7) 南 回 帰 線 (Tropic of Capricorn)
   みなみかいきせん
   minami kaikisen

8) 南 極 点 (South Pole)
   なんきょくてん
   nankyoku ten

9) 北 極 点 (North Pole)
   ほっきょくてん
   hakkyoku ten

10) 北 極 圏 (Arctic Circle)
    ほっきょくけん
    hokkyoku ken

11) 大 陸 (continent)
    たいりく
    tairiku

12) 海 外 (overseas)
    かいがい
    kaigai

13) アフリカ (Africa)
    afurika

14) アジア (Asia)
    ajia

15) 北 アメリカ (North America)
    きた
    kita amerika

16) 中 央 アメリカ (Central America)
    ちゅうおう
    chuuou amerika

17) 南 アメリカ (South America)
    みなみ
    minami amerika

18) ヨーロッパ (Europe)
    yooroppa

19) オセアニア (Oceania)
    oseania

20) 南 極 (Antarctica)
    なんきょく
    nankyoku

21) 経 線 (meridian)
    けいせん
    keisen

22) 緯 線 (parallel)
    いせん
    isen

23) 大 西 洋 (Atlantic Ocean)
    たいせいよう
    taiseiyou

24) 太 平 洋 (Pacific Ocean)
    たいへいよう
    taiheiyou

東 京 の 南 に住んでいます。*Tokyo no minami ni sundeimasu.* I live in the south of Tokyo.
とうきょう みなみ す

大 西 洋 でサーフィンするのが大好きです。*Taiseiyou de saafin suru noga daisuki desu.*
たいせいよう だいす
I love to surf in the Atlantic Ocean.

ヨーロッパへ旅 行 する予定です。*Yooroppa he ryokou suru yotei desu.*
りょこう よてい
We have planned a trip to Europe.

116

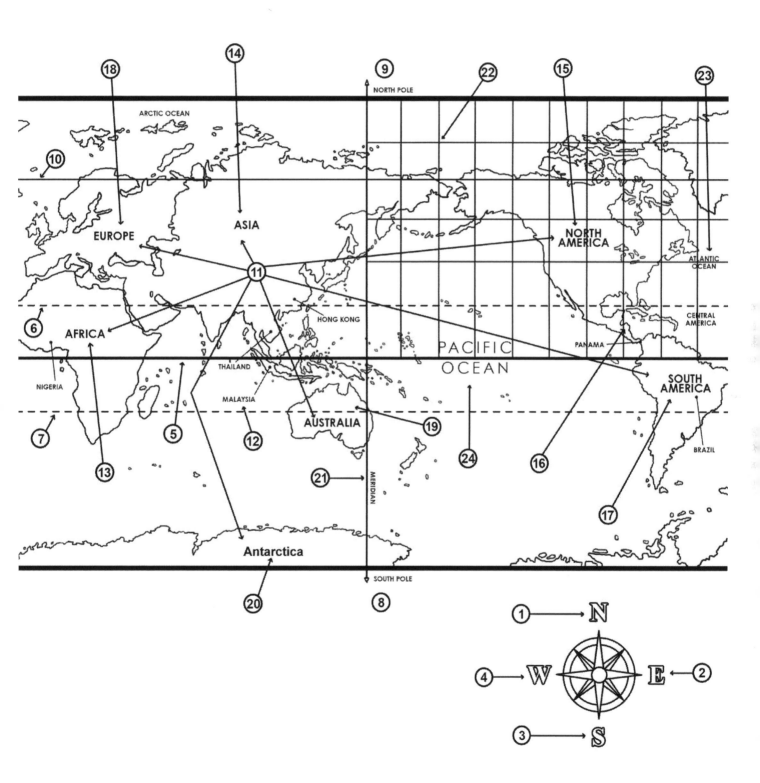

病院 (THE HOSPITAL)

1) 医者 (doctor/medic)
isha

2) 看護師 (nurse)
kangoshi

3) 救急車 (ambulance)
kyuukyuusha

4) 救急箱 (first-aid kit)
kyuukyuubako

5) 体温計 (thermometer)
taionkei

6) 担架 (stretcher)
tanka

7) 注射器 (syringe)
chuushaki

8) 針 (needle)
hari

9) 聴診器 (stethoscope)
choushinki

10) 松葉杖 (crutches)
matsubazue

11) 車椅子 (wheelchair)
kuruma isu

12) 観察室 (observation room)
kansatsu shitsu

13) 病床 (hospital bed)
byoushou

14) 注射 (injection)
chuusha

15) 手術 (surgery)
shujutsu

16) 病歴 (medical history)
byoureki

17) 患者 (patient)
kanja

18) 錠剤 (pill/tablet)
jouzai

水曜日にお医者さんの予約があります。 *Suiyoubi ni oishasan no yoyaku ga arimasu.*
I have an appointment with the doctor on Wednesday.

私が車椅子を押せますよ。 *Watashi ga kurumaisu wo osemasuyo.*
I can push your wheelchair.

娘は看護師になりたがっています。 *Musume wa kangoshi ni naritagatteimasu.*
My daughter wants to become a nurse.

118

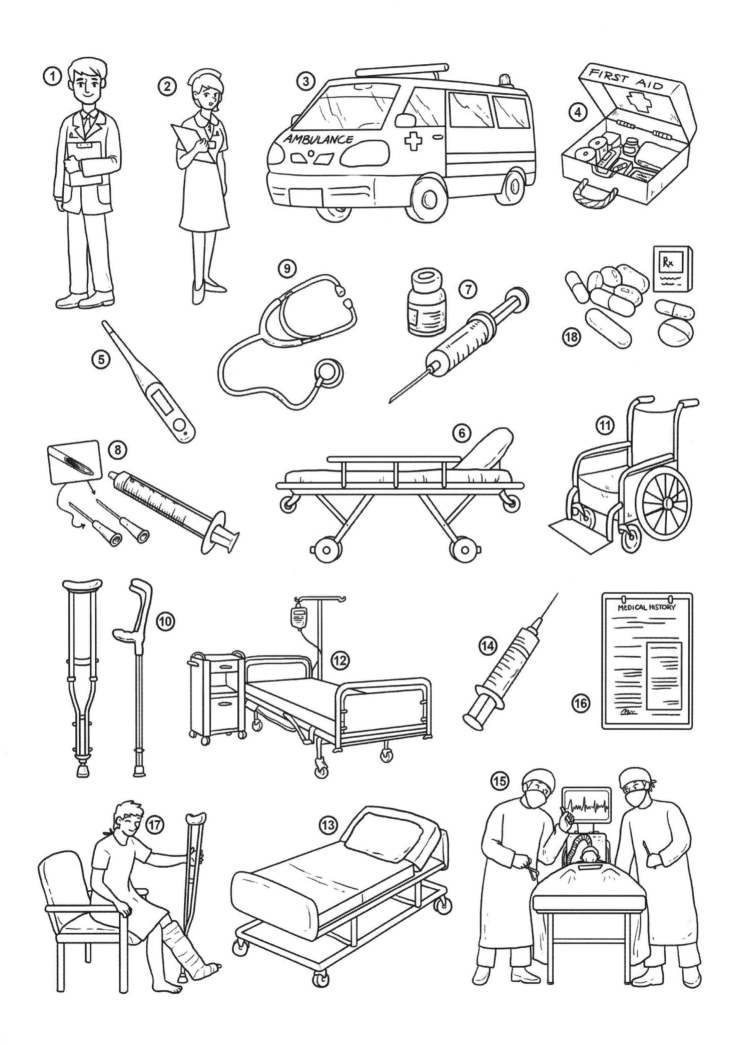

農場 (THE FARM)

1) 納屋 (barn)
naya

2) 牛小屋 (cowshed/stable)
ushi goya

3) 農家 (farmer)
nouka

4) すき (plough)
suki

5) サイロ (silo)
sairo

6) 風車 (mill)
fuusha

7) 水おけ (water trough)
mizuoke

8) 鶏小屋 (henhouse)
niwatori goya

9) はちの巣 (beehive)
hachi no su

10) 干し草 (hay bale)
hoshikusa

11) 畜牛 (cattle)
chikugyuu

12) 乳搾り (to milk)
chichishibori

13) 群れ (herd/flock)
mure

14) 雌鶏／鶏 (hen)
mendori/niwatori

15) 井戸 (well)
ido

16) かんがいシステム (irrigation system)
kangai shisutemu

17) かかし (scarecrow)
kakashi

18) 砂利道 (dirt road)
jarimichi

私の鶏は一日１２個の卵を産みます。*Watashi no niwatori wa ichinichi juuni ko no tamago wo umimasu.*
My hens lay a dozen eggs per day.

鳥を追い払うために、畑にかかしをつけました。*Tori wo oiharau tameni, hatake ni kakashi wo tsukemashita.*
I installed a scarecrow in my field to scare birds away.

左に曲がって、砂利道をまっすぐ行ってください。*Hidari ni magatte, jarimichi wo massugu itte kudasai.*
Turn left and follow the dirt road.

QUIZ #5

Use arrows to match the corresponding translations:

a. laboratory

b. pear

c. drums

d. north

e. well

f. bagpipes

g. wheelchair

h. henhouse

i. eggplant

j. nurse

k. Earth

l. cauliflower

m. strawberry

n. flash drive

o. statistics

p. cherry

1. 車椅子 (くるまいす)

2. 井戸 (いど)

3. 鶏小屋 (にわとりごや)

4. ナス

5. 地球 (ちきゅう)

6. ドラム

7. 研究室 (けんきゅうしつ)

8. ナシ

9. カリフラワー

10. イチゴ

11. 北 (きた)

12. バグパイプ

13. 看護師 (かんごし)

14. 統計値 (とうけいち)

15. チェリー

16. フラッシュドライブ

Fill in the blank spaces with the options below (use each word only once):

私のおじいちゃんは＿＿＿＿＿をしています。

牛や羊をたくさん飼っています。また＿＿＿＿＿や＿＿＿＿＿などの野菜も育てています。

私は毎年夏に遊びに行って、＿＿＿＿＿をしたり＿＿＿＿＿のそうじを手伝います。

田舎なので、空気もきれいです。夜は＿＿＿＿＿が見えることもあります。

夜はお茶を飲みながら、＿＿＿＿＿を弾いてくれます。

でも去年は病気になり、一度＿＿＿＿＿で病院へ運ばれて、＿＿＿＿＿を受けました。

今でもときどき＿＿＿＿＿に行きますが、すっかりよくなりました。

アコースティックギター

牛小屋

救急車

流れ星

乳搾り

じゃがいも

農家

たまねぎ

手術

お医者さん

食べ物 (FOOD)

1) レーズン (grape)
   reezun

2) クルミ (walnuts)
   kurumi

3) 肉 (meat)
   niku

4) ラム肉 (lamb)
   ramuniku

5) 魚 (fish)
   sakana

6) 鶏肉 (chicken)
   toriniku

7) ターキー (turkey)
   taakii

8) はちみつ (honey)
   hachimitsu

9) 砂糖 (sugar)
   satou

10) 塩 (salt)
    shio

11) こしょう (pepper)
    koshou

12) ベーコン (bacon)
    beekon

13) ソーセージ (sausages)
    souseeji

14) ケチャップ (ketchup)
    kechappu

15) マヨネーズ (mayonnaise)
    mayoneezu

16) からし (mustard)
    karashi

17) ジャム (jam)
    jamu

18) バター (butter)
    bataa

19) ジュース (juice)
    juusu

20) 牛乳 (milk)
    gyuunyuu

マヨネーズなしでフライドポテトは食べられません。 *Mayoneezu nashi de furaido poteto wa taberaremasen.*

I cannot eat fries without mayonnaise.

ハチは、はちみつを作ります。 *Hachi wa, hachimitsu wo tsukurimasu.*

Bees make honey.

鶏肉と魚、どちらがいいですか? *Toriniku to sakana, dochira ga iidesuka?*

Do you prefer chicken or fish?

124

料理 (DISHES)
<small>りょうり</small>

1) ラザニア (lasagna)
   razania

2) オムレツ (omelette)
   omuretsu

3) ミートローフ (meatloaf)
   miito roofu

4) 焼きそば (fried noodles)
   <small>や</small>
   yakisoba

5) マカロニアンドチーズ(macaroni and cheese)
   makaroni ando chiizu

6) パエリア (paella)
   paeria

7) バーベキューリブ (barbecue ribs)
   baabekyuu ribu

8) コーンブレッド (cornbread)
   koon bureddo

9) 春巻 (spring roll)
   <small>はるまき</small>
   harumaki

10) チーズバーガー (cheeseburger)
    chiizu baagaa

11) フライドチキン (fried chicken)
    furaido chikin

12) シーザーサラダ (Caesar salad)
    shiizaa sarada

13) オニオンスープ (onion soup)
    onion suupu

14) コールスロー (coleslaw)
    kooru suroo

15) 手羽先 (chicken wings)
    <small>てばさき</small>
    tebasaki

16) チョコチップケーキ (chocolate-chip cookies)
    chokochippu keeki

17) レモンパイ (key lime pie)
    kii raimu pai

18) チーズケーキ (cheesecake)
    chiizu keeki

アメリカ人はマカロニアンドチーズが大好きです。 *Amerika jin wa makaroni ando chiizu ga daisuki desu.*
Americans love macaroni and cheese.

オニオンスープを注文します。 *Onion suupu wo chuumon shimasu.*
I am going to order the onion soup.

チーズケーキは私の好きなデザートです。 *Chiizu keeki wa watashi no sukina dezaato desu.*
Cheesecake is my favorite dessert.

シーフード (SEAFOOD)

1) アンチョビ (anchovy)
anchobi

2) タラ (cod)
tara

3) タラバガニ (Red king crab)
tarabagani

4) サバ (mackerel)
saba

5) ロブスター (lobster)
robusutaa

6) ホタテ (scallop)
hotate

7) フエダイ (snapper)
fuedai

8) いくら (salmon roe)
ikura

9) カニ (crab)
kani

10) ムールがい (mussel)
muurugai

11) うなぎ (eel)
unagi

12) エビ (shrimp)
ebi

ピザにアンチョビをのせたいです。 *Piza ni anchobi wo nosetai desu.*
I want anchovies on my pizza.

ホタテはとても高いです。 *Hotate wa totemo takai desu.*
Scallops are very expensive.

日本人は生のいくらをごはんと一緒に食べます。 *Nihon jin wa nama no ikura wo gohan to isshoni tabemasu.*
Japanese people eat raw salmon roe with rice.

形 (SHAPES)
かたち

1) 円 (circle)
えん
en

2) だ円 (oval)
えん
daen

3) 三角 (triangle)
さんかく
sankaku

4) 長方形 (rectangle)
ちょうほうけい
chouhoukei

5) 四角 (square)
しかく
shikaku

6) 台形 (trapezoid)
だいけい
daikei

7) ひし形 (rhombus)
がた
hishigata

8) 立方体 (cube)
りっぽうたい
rippoutai

9) 五角形 (pentagon)
ごかっけい
gokakkei

10) 六角形 (hexagon)
ろっかくけい
rokkakkei

11) 矢印 (arrow)
やじるし
yajirushi

12) 十字 (cross)
じゅうじ
juuji

13) ハート (heart)
haato

14) 星 (star)
ほし
hoshi

15) 円柱 (cylinder)
えんちゅう
enchuu

16) 円すい (cone)
えん
ensui

17) ピラミッド (pyramid)
piramiddo

18) 球体 (sphere)
きゅうたい
kyuutai

19) 角柱 (prism)
かくちゅう
kakuchuu

エジプトのピラミッドを見たことがありますか？ *Ejiputo no piramiddo wo mita kotoga arimasuka?* Have you ever seen the pyramids in Egypt?

博物館の入り口に行くには、矢印に沿って進んでください。 *Hakubutsukan no iriguchi ni iku niwa, yajirushi ni sotte susunde kudasai.*
To find the entrance of the museum, please follow arrows provided.

地球は球体で、平らじゃないです。 *Chikyuu wa kyuutai de, tairajanai desu.*
The earth is a sphere, not flat.

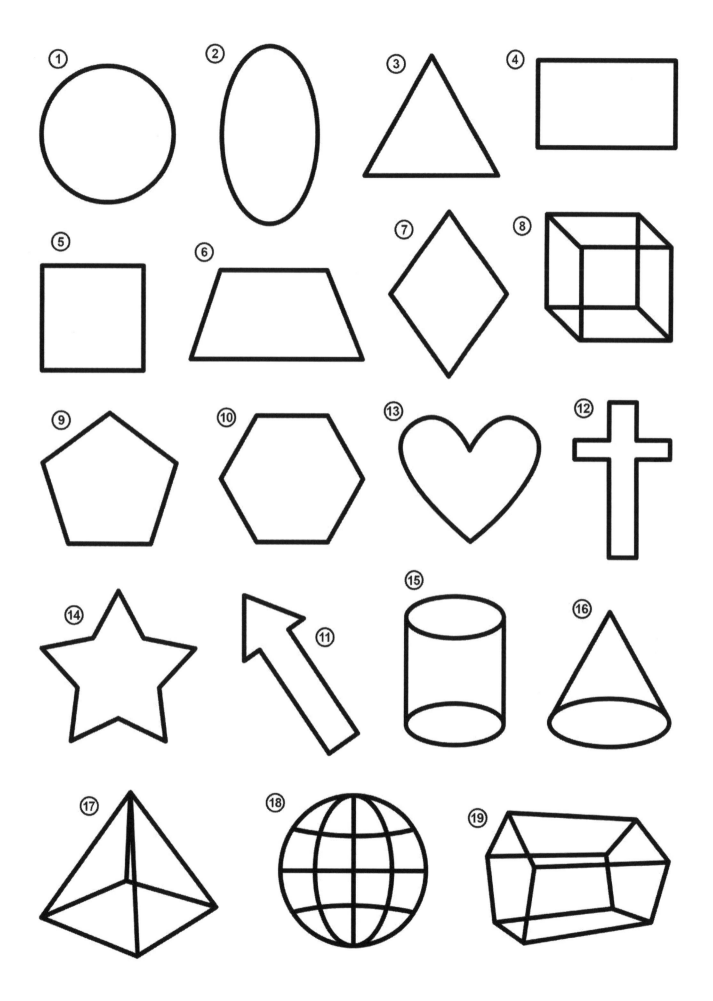

スーパー (THE SUPERMARKET)

1) ショッピングカート (shopping cart)
shoppingu kaato

2) 商品棚 (cabinet/display case)
しょうひんだな
shouhindana

3) お客さん (customer)
きゃく
okyaku san

4) レジ係 (cashier)
がかり
reji gakari

5) レシート (receipt)
reshiito

6) パン屋 (bakery)
や
panya

7) フルーツと野菜 (fruits and
やさい
vegetables)
furuutsu to yasai

8) 肉 (meat)
にく
niku

9) 乳製品 (dairy products)
にゅうせいひん
nyuusei hin

10) 魚 (fish)
さかな
sakana

11) 冷凍食品 (frozen food)
れいとうしょくひん
reitou shokuhin

12) 鶏肉 (poultry)
とりにく
toriniku

13) 豆 (legumes)
まめ
mame

14) お菓子 (snacks)
かし
okashi

15) デザート (dessert)
dezaato

16) 飲み物 (drinks)
の もの
nomimono

17) 日用雑貨 (household items)
にちようざっか
nichiyouzakka

18) ベルトコンベアー (belt conveyor)
beruto konbeaa

毎朝パン屋へパンを買いに行きます。 *Maiasa panya e pan wo kaini ikimasu.*
まいあさ   や   か い
I go to the bakery to get bread every morning.

私はベジタリアンなので、肉は食べません。 *Watashi wa bejitarian nanode, niku wa tabemasen.*
わたし   にく た
I am a vegetarian; I do not eat meat.

このお店はフルーツと野菜の品揃えがいい。 *Kono omise wa furuutsu to yasai no shinazoroe ga*
みせ   やさい しなぞろ
ii.
This shop has a great selection of fruits and vegetables.

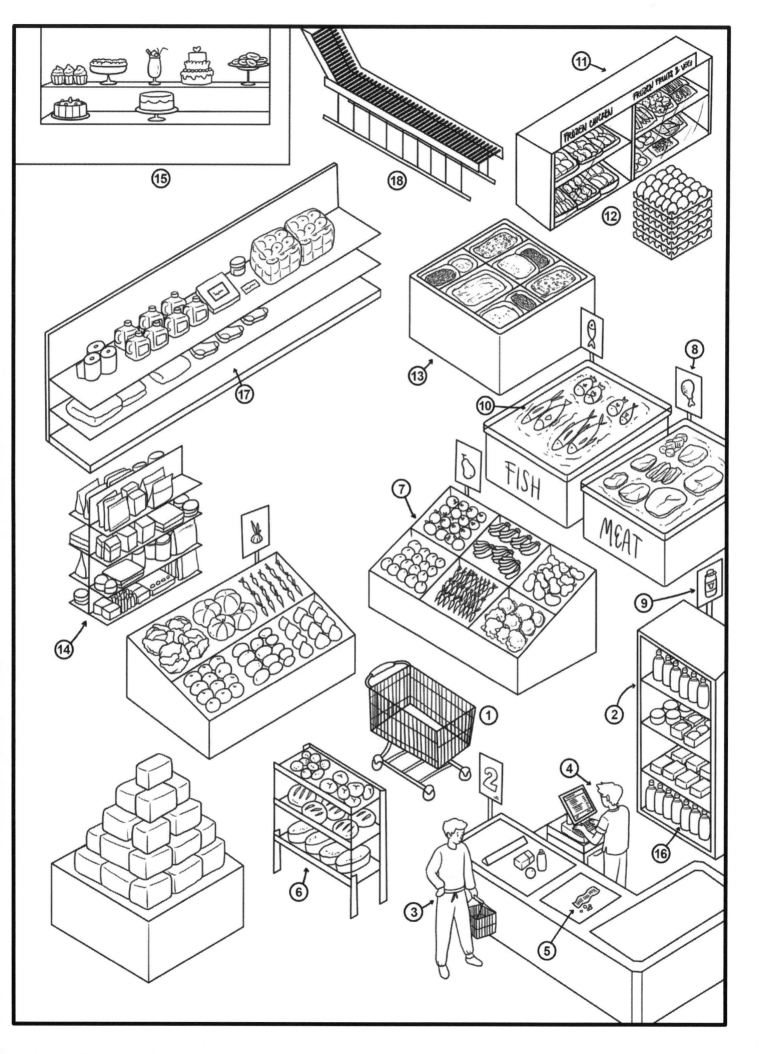

FROZEN CHICKEN

FROZEN FRUITS & VEG

FISH

MEAT

マスメディア (MEDIA)

1) 雑誌 (magazine)
ざっし
zasshi

2) ファックス (fax)
fakkusu

3) 新聞 (journal)
しんぶん
shinbun

4) 郵便 (postal mail)
ゆうびん
yuubin

5) 手紙 (letter)
てがみ
tegami

6) ラジオ (radio)
rajio

7) まんが (comic)
manga

8) 本 (book)
ほん
hon

9) 写真 (photography)
しゃしん
shashin

10) 固定電話 (landline phone)
こていでんわ
kotei denwa

11) テレビ (TV)
terebi

12) 映画 (movies)
えいが
eiga

13) 携帯電話 (mobile phone/cell phone)
けいたいでんわ
keitai denwa

14) 手話 (sign language)
しゅわ
shuwa

明日の夜、テレビでビヨンセのコンサートが放送されます。 *Asu no yoru, terebi de biyonse no konsaato ga housou saremasu.*
あした よる ほうそう
Beyoncé's concert airs on TV tomorrow night.

携帯電話の番号をくれませんか。 *Keitaidenwa no bangou wo kuremasenka.*
けいたいでんわ ばんごう
Can you give me your cell number?

彼に手紙を送りました。 *Kare ni tegami wo okurimashita.*
かれ てがみ おく
I have sent him a letter.

遊園地 (THE FAIR/THE AMUSEMENT PARK)

1) ミラーハウス (house of mirrors)
   miraa hausu

2) 海賊船 (pirate ship/boat swing)
   kaizoku sen

3) 切符売り場 (ticket booth)
   kippu uriba

4) 回転ブランコ (swing ride)
   kaiten buranko

5) ローラーコースター (roller coaster)
   rooraa koosutaa

6) 観覧車 (Ferris wheel)
   kanransha

7) メリーゴーランド (carousel/merry-go-round)
   merii goo rando

8) バンパーカー (bumper cars)
   banpaa kaa

9) コーヒーカップ (teacups/cup and saucer)
   koohii kappu

10) 振り子 (pendulum)
    furiko

11) ゲームセンター (arcade room)
    geemu sentaa

12) アメリカンドッグ (corn dog)
    amerikan doggu

13) スノーコーン (snow cone)
    sunoo koon

14) 綿菓子 (cotton candy)
    watagashi

15) リンゴあめ (candy apple)
    ringo ame

ローラーコースターが大好きです。 *Rooraa koosutaa ga daisuki desu.*
I love roller coasters.

彼はミラーハウスで迷った。 *Kare wa miraa hausu de mayotta.*
He got lost in the house of mirrors.

綿菓子を食べ過ぎてしまった。 *Watagashi wo tabesugite shimatta.*
I ate too much cotton candy.

人生の出来事 (LIFE EVENTS)

1) 誕生 (birth)
tanjou

2) 洗礼 (christening/baptism)
senrei

3) 始業式 (first day of school)
shigyoushiki

4) 友達をつくる (to make friends)
tomodachi wo tsukuru

5) 誕生日 (birthday)
tanjoubi

6) 恋に落ちる (to fall in love)
koi ni ochiru

7) 卒業 (graduation)
sotsugyou

8) 大学に入る (to enter a university)
daigaku ni hairu

9) 就職する (to get a job)
shyushokusuru

10) 起業家になる (to become an entrepreneur)
kigyouka ni naru

11) 世界中を旅行する (to travel around the world)
seikai juu wo ryokousuru

12) 結婚する (to get married)
kekkonsuru

13) 子供を持つ (to have a baby)
kodomo wo motsu

14) 誕生日を祝う (to celebrate a birthday)
tanjoubi wo iwau

15) 退職 (retirement)
taishoku

16) 死 (death)
shi

来月結婚します。 *Raigetsu kekkon shimasu.*
I am going to get married next month.

両親は退職しました。 *Ryoushin wa taishoku shimashita.*
My parents are retired.

真司はやっと仕事を見つけました。 *Shinji wa yatto shigoto wo mitsukemashita.*
Shinji has finally found a job.

形容詞 I (ADJECTIVES I)

1) 大きい (big)
ookii

2) 小さい (small)
chiisai

3) うるさい (loud)
urusai

4) 静かな (silent)
shizukana

5) 長い (long)
nagai

6) 短い (short)
mijikai

7) 広い (wide)
hiroi

8) 狭い (narrow)
semai

9) 高い (expensive)
takai

10) 安い (cheap)
yasui

11) 速い (fast)
hayai

12) 遅い (slow)
osoi

13) 空 (empty)
kara

14) いっぱい (full)
ippai

15) 柔らかい (soft)
yawarakai

16) 硬い (hard)
katai

17) 高い (tall)
takai

18) 低い (short)
hikui

近所の犬はとてもうるさい。 *Kinjo no inu wa totemo urusai.*
The neighbor's dog is very loud.

このレストランはおいしくて安い。 *Kono resutoran wa oishikute yasui.*
This restaurant is good and cheap.

弟は私より背が高い。 *Otouto wa watashi yori se ga takai.*
My young brother is taller than me.

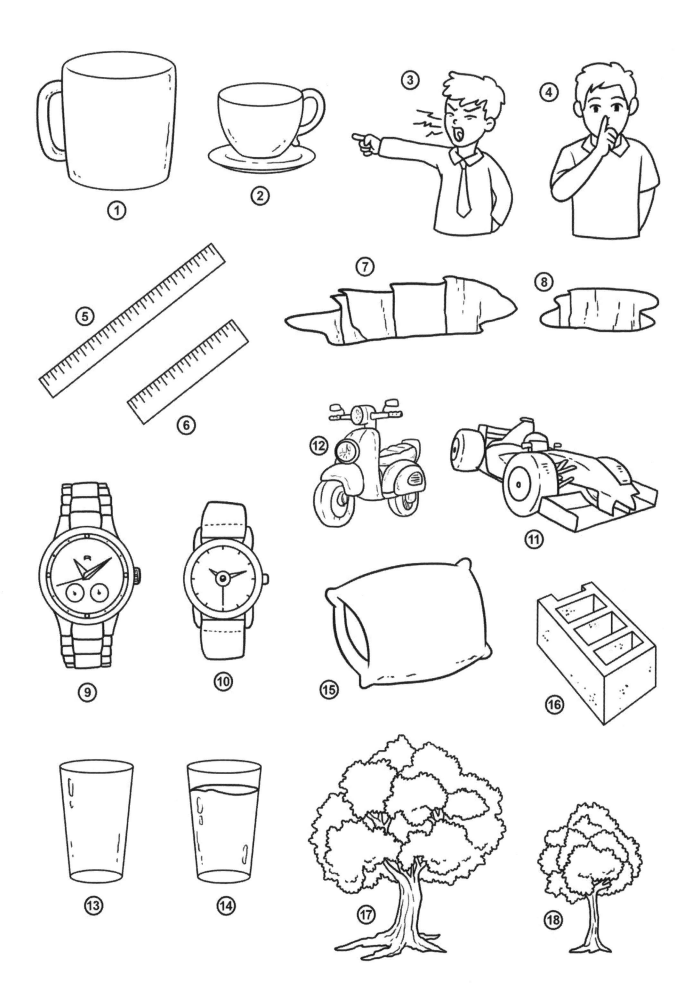

QUIZ #6

Use arrows to match the corresponding translations:

a. book

b. dairy products

c. roller coaster

d. eel

e. circle

f. anchovy

g. jam

h. cotton candy

i. carousel

j. turkey

k. drinks

l. cross

m. walnuts

n. fish

o. onion soup

p. arrow

1. ジャム

2. アンチョビ

3. うなぎ

4. <ruby>魚<rt>さかな</rt></ruby>

5. ターキー

6. <ruby>飲<rt>の</rt></ruby>み<ruby>物<rt>もの</rt></ruby>

7. <ruby>乳製品<rt>にゅうせいひん</rt></ruby>

8. <ruby>円<rt>えん</rt></ruby>

9. ローラーコースター

10. くるみ

11. <ruby>本<rt>ほん</rt></ruby>

12. <ruby>矢印<rt>やじるし</rt></ruby>

13. オニオンスープ

14. <ruby>十字<rt>じゅうじ</rt></ruby>

15. メリーゴーランド

16. <ruby>綿菓子<rt>わたがし</rt></ruby>

Fill in the blank spaces with the options below (use each word only once):

高校の＿＿＿＿＿式のあと、家族と遊園地にいきました。

弟と私は＿＿＿＿＿＿に乗りました。おかあさんは＿＿＿＿＿ところが苦手なのでおとうさんと＿＿＿＿＿＿に乗りました。お昼ごはんは＿＿＿＿＿＿を食べました。おかあさんはベジタリアンなので＿＿＿＿＿を食べていました。来月は＿＿＿＿＿＿＿。

おかあさんは私に「大学でなにをしたいの？」と聞きました。私は「＿＿＿＿＿＿＿＿」と答えました。みんな笑っていました。でも本気なんです。お金を稼いだり、ことにはあまり興味がありません。旅の途中で外国人の女の子と＿＿＿＿＿＿かも！

起業家になる　　　　　　　　　世界中を旅行する

高い　　　　　　　　　　　　　シーザーサラダ

卒業　　　　　　　　　　　　　ローラーコースター

チーズバーガー　　　　　　　　大学に入ります

結婚する　　　　　　　　　　　メリーゴーランド

143

形容詞 II (ADJECTIVES II)

1) 新しい (new)
atarashii

2) 古い (old)
furui

3) 快適な (comfortable)
kaitekina

4) 落ち着かない (uncomfortable)
ochitsukanai

5) 危ない (dangerous)
abunai

6) イライラする (annoying)
iraira suru

7) 震える (shaky)
furueru

8) 完全な (complete)
kanzenna

9) 不完全な (incomplete)
fukanzenna

10) 壊れた (broken)
kowareta

11) 美しい (gorgeous)
utsukushii

12) 高潔な (virtuous)
kouketsuna

13) 似ている (similar)
niteiru

14) 違う (different)
chigau

15) 開いている (open)
aiteiru

16) 閉じている / 閉まっている (closed)
tojiteiru / shimatteiru

この双子はよく似ている。 *Kono futago wa yoku niteiru.*
Those twins are very similar.

私のソファーは古いけど快適です。 *Watashi no sofaa wa furui kedo kaiteki desu.*
My sofa is old but comfortable.

今日は祝日で、銀行は閉まっている。 *Kyou wa shukujitsu de, ginkou wa shimatteiru.*
Today is a holiday and the banks are closed!

144

副詞 (ADVERBS)

ふくし

1) ここ (here)
   koko

2) そこ (there)
   soko

3) 近く (near)
   ちか
   chikaku

4) 遠く (far)
   とお
   tooku

5) 上 (up)
   うえ
   ue

6) 下 (down)
   した
   shita

7) 中 (inside)
   なか
   naka

8) 外 (outside)
   そと
   soto

9) 前 (ahead)
   まえ
   mae

10) 後ろ (behind)
    うし
    ushiro

11) いいえ (no)
    iie

12) はい (yes)
    hai

13) 今 (now)
    いま
    ima

14) いい / 正しい (well/good/right)
    ただ
    ii / tadashii

15) 悪い / 間違い (bad/wrong)
    わる   まちが
    warui / machigai

下で待っています。 *Shita de matteimasu.*
した　ま
I am waiting for you downstairs.

今電話してください。 *Ima denwa shite kudasai.*
いまでんわ
Call me now.

ここで食べますか？むこうで食べますか？ *Koko de tabemasuka ? Mukou de tabemasuka ?*
た　　　　　　　た
Are we eating here or over there?

方角 (DIRECTIONS)
<ruby>方角<rt>ほうがく</rt></ruby> (DIRECTIONS)

1) ブロック (block)
   burokku

2) 広場 (square)
   hiroba

3) 公園 (park)
   kouen

4) 地下鉄 (subway)
   chikatetsu

5) 角 (corner)
   kado

6) 通り (avenue)
   toori

7) 道 (street)
   michi

8) バス停 (bus stop)
   basutei

9) 信号機 (traffic light)
   shingouki

10) 横断歩道 (crossing/crosswalk)
    oudan hodou

11) 上 (up)
    ue

12) 下 (down)
    shita

13) 左 (left)
    hidari

14) 右 (right)
    migi

15) 道路標識 (road sign)
    douro hyoushiki

16) 交通警察 (traffic police)
    koutsuu keisatsu

地下鉄の臭いが好きじゃない。 *Chikatetsu no nioi ga sukijanai.*
I do not like the smell of the subway.

バス停はどこですか。 *Basutei wa doko desuka.*
Where is the bus stop?

横断歩道を使わなきゃいけません。 *Oudan hodou wo tsukawanakya ikemasen.*
You must use the crosswalk.

レストラン (THE RESTAURANT)

1) マネージャー (manager)
maneejaa

2) テーブル (table)
teeburu

3) メニュー (menu)
menyuu

4) お皿 (dish)
osara

5) アペタイザー (appetizer)
apetaizaa

6) 前菜 (starter)
zensai

7) メインコース (main course)
mein koosu

8) デザート (dessert)
dezaato

9) 夜ごはん (dinner)
yoru gohan

10) コック (cook)
kokku

11) ウェイター (waiter)
weitaa

12) ウェイトレス (waitress)
weitoresu

13) チップ (tip)
chippu

14) ハイチェア (high chair)
haichea

15) ワインリスト (wine list)
wain risuto

16) パティシエ (pastry chef)
patishie

メニューをください。 *Menyuu wo kudasai.*
Can I have the menu?

アペタイザーをください。 *Apetaizaa wo kudasai.*
I will have an appetizer please.

デザートは何にしますか。 *Dezaato wa nani ni shimasuka.*
What would you like to have for dessert ?

ショッピングモール (THE MALL)

1) 階 / 床 (floor)
かい / ゆか
kai / yuka

2) 水族館 (aquarium)
すいぞくかん
suizokukan

3) フードコート (food court)
fuudo kooto

4) エレベーター (elevator)
erebeetaa

5) エスカレーター (escalators)
esukareetaa

6) 非常口 (emergency exit)
ひじょうぐち
hijouguchi

7) 美容院 (beauty salon)
びよういん
biyouin

8) アパレルショップ (clothing store)
apareru shoppu

9) 遊び場 (playground)
あそ び
asobiba

10) 警備員 (security guard)
けいびいん
keibiin

11) 監視カメラ (surveillance camera)
かんし
kanshi kamera

12) パン屋 (bakery)
や
panya

13) スポーツ用品店 (sports store)
ようひんてん
supootsu youhinten

14) 噴水 (fountain)
ふんすい
funsui

エレベーターを使って、2階で止まってください。*Erebeetaa wo tsukatte, nikai de tomatte kudasai.*
Take the elevator and stop on the second floor.

息子を遊び場に連れていきます。*Musuko wo asobiba ni tsurete ikimasu.*
I am going to take my son to the playground.

スポーツ用品店の隣りに住んでいます。*Supootsu youhinten no tonari ni sundeimasu.*
I live next to the sports store.

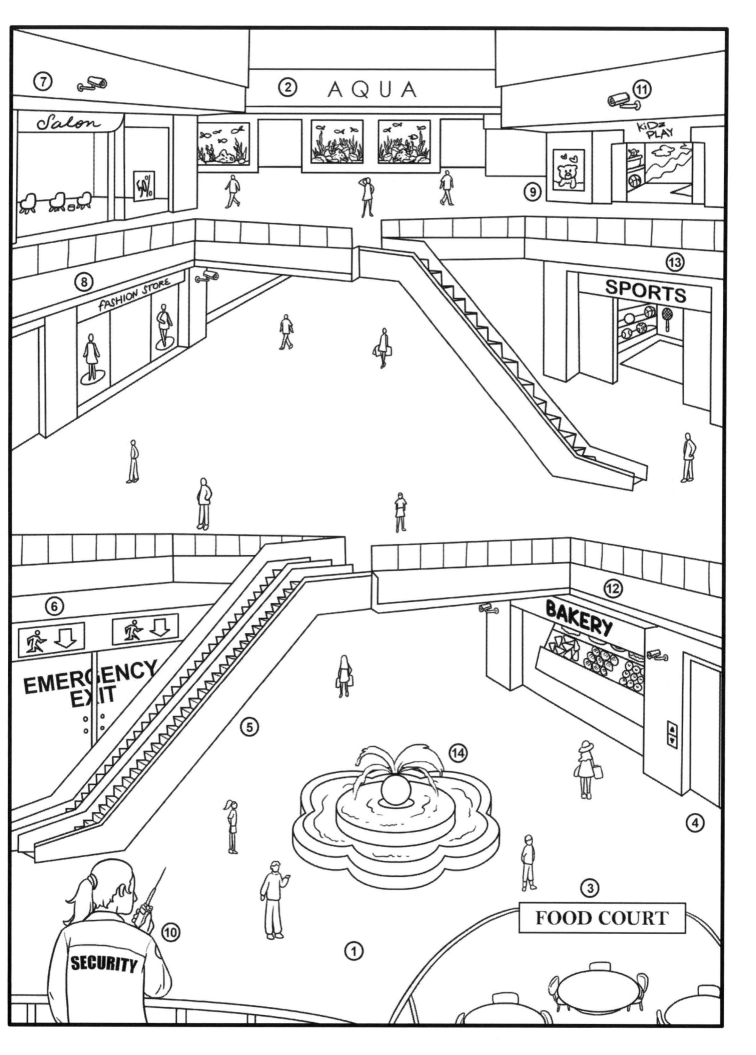

動詞 I (VERBS I)

1) 話す (to talk)
   hanasu

2) 飲む (to drink)
   nomu

3) 食べる (to eat)
   taberu

4) 歩く (to walk)
   aruku

5) 開ける (to open)
   akeru

6) 閉める (to close)
   shimeru

7) あげる (to give)
   ageru

8) 見る (to see)
   miru

9) ついていく (to follow)
   tsuiteiku

10) 抱きしめる (to hug)
    dakishimeru

11) キスする (to kiss)
    kisu suru

12) 買う (to buy)
    kau

13) 聴く (to listen)
    kiku

14) 歌う (to sing)
    utau

15) 踊る (to dance)
    odoru

窓を閉めてください。 *Mado wo shimete kudasai.*
Please close the window.

私についてきて！ *Watashi ni tsuite kite！*
Follow me!

彼に１０００円あげました。 *Kare ni sen en agemashita.*
I gave him 1000 yen.

動詞 II (VERBS II)

1) 書く (to write)
kaku

2) 読む (to read)
yomu

3) 掃除する (to clean)
souji suru

4) 拾う (to pick up)
hirou

5) 見つける (to find)
mitsukeru

6) 洗う (to wash)
arau

7) 見る (to watch)
miru

8) 直す (to fix)
naosu

9) 思う (to think)
omou

10) 取る (to take)
toru

11) 切る (to cut)
kiru

12) 止まる (to stop)
tomaru

13) 泣く (to cry)
naku

14) 笑う (to smile)
warau

15) 助ける (to help)
tasukeru

サンディは月曜日に自分の部屋を掃除します。 *Sandi wa getsuyoubi ni jibun no heya wo souji shimasu.*

Sandy cleans her room on Monday.

車を洗います。 *Kuruma wo araimasu.*

I am going to wash my car.

それは良いアイディアだと思う。 *Sore wa yoi aidia dato omou.*

I think that is a good idea.

156

工事 I (CONSTRUCTION I)

1) クレーン (crane)
kureen

2) 立ち入り禁止テープ (hazard tape)
tachiiri kinshi teepu

3) トラフィックコーン (traffic cone)
torafikku koon

4) シャベル (construction shovel)
shaberu

5) ハンマー (hammer)
hanmaa

6) ワイヤカッター (wire cutters)
waiya kattaa

7) ペイントローラー (paint roller)
peinto rooraa

8) チェーンソー (chainsaw)
cheensoo

9) 電動ドリル (drill)
dendou doriru

10) ジャックハンマー (jackhammer)
jakku hanmaa

11) ペンチ (pliers)
penchi

12) スクリュードライバー (screwdriver)
sukuryuu doraibaa

チェーンソーはとてもうるさい。 *Cheensoo wa totemo urusai.*
The chainsaw is very loud.

この写真を掛けるのにハンマーがいります。 *Kono shashin wo kakeru noni hanmaa ga irimasu.*
I need a hammer to hang this picture.

スクリュードライバーをください。 *Sukuryuu doraibaa wo kudasai.*
Give me the screwdriver.

158

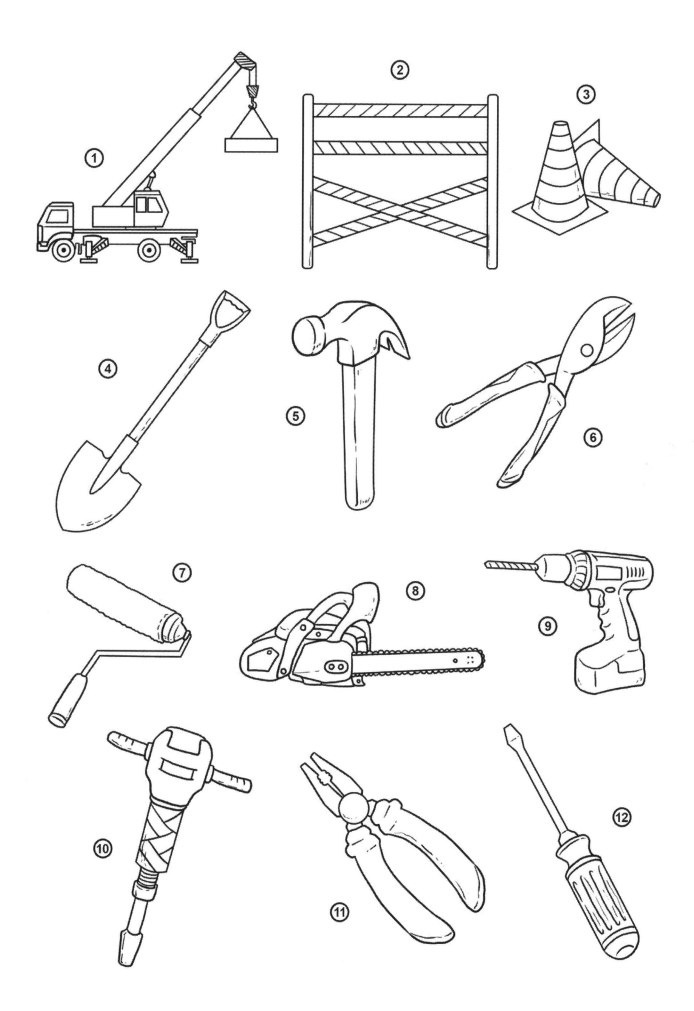

工事 II (CONSTRUCTION II)

1) ツールボックス (toolbox)
   tuuru bokkusu

2) 作業用ヘルメット (work helmet/hard hat)
   sagyouyou herumetto

3) 設計図 (blueprint)
   sekkeizu

4) パイプ (pipes)
   paipu

5) こて (trowel)
   kote

6) コンクリートミキサー (concrete mixer)
   konkuriito mikisaa

7) れんが (brick)
   renga

8) 建築材料 (building materials)
   kenchiku zairyou

9) タイル (tiles)
   tairu

10) セメント (cement)
    semento

11) 砂 (sand)
    suna

12) 砂利 (gravel)
    jari

イギリスの家はれんがでできています。 *Igirisu no ie wa renga de dekiteimasu.*
English houses are made of bricks.

私のツールボックスはガレージにあります。 *Watashi no tsuurubokkusu wa gareeji ni arimasu.*
My toolbox is in the garage.

工事現場では作業用ヘルメットを被らなきゃいけません。 *Koujigenba dewa sagyouyou herumetto wo kaburanakya ikemasen.*
You must wear the work helmet in the construction site.

QUIZ #7

Use arrows to match the corresponding translations:

a. waitress

b. left

c. old

d. bus stop

e. bad

f. playground

g. right

h. to talk

i. main course

j. closed

k. to sing

l. elevator

m. to buy

n. open

o. bakery

p. far

1. ウェイトレス

2. 古い

3. 遊び場

4. 右

5. 歌う

6. 買う

7. 左

8. バス停

9. エレベーター

10. 話す

11. 開いている

12. 悪い

13. 遠く

14. パン屋

15. 閉まっている

16. メインコース

Fill in the blank spaces with the options below (use each word only once):

昨日サンディと一緒に＿＿＿＿＿＿レストランに行きました。＿＿＿＿＿＿に乗って１０分ほどの場所です。大きな＿＿＿＿＿＿の前にあります。レストランの椅子は柔らかく、とてもでした。

まずは＿＿＿＿＿＿を呼んで、ワインを注文しました。＿＿＿＿＿＿はビーフステーキです。＿＿＿＿＿＿にチーズケーキを＿＿＿＿＿＿。とてもおいしかったです。

良いサービスだったので＿＿＿＿＿＿をたくさん払いました。そのあと、二人で町をすこし＿＿＿＿＿＿。

歩きました

チップ

地下鉄

メインコース

広場

食べました

新しい

ウェイター

デザート

快適

163

植物と木 (PLANTS AND TREES)

1) 野生の花 (wildflower)
   yasei no hana

2) ハーブ (herb)
   haabu

3) マッシュルーム (mushroom)
   masshu ruumu

4) 雑草 (weed)
   zassou

5) 海草 (seaweed)
   kaisou

6) シダ (fern)
   shida

7) アシ (reed)
   ashi

8) 竹 (bamboo)
   take

9) ツタ (ivy)
   tsuta

10) コケ (moss)
    koke

11) 草 (grass)
    kusa

12) ヤシの木 (palm tree)
    yashi no ki

13) マングローブ (mangrove)
    manguroobu

14) サボテン (cactus)
    saboten

寝る前にハーブティーを飲むのが好きです。 *Neru maeni haabutii wo nomu noga suki desu.*
I like to drink herbal tea before I go to bed.

竹は伸びるのがとても速い。 *Take wa nobiru noga totemo hayai.*
Bamboo grows very fast.

サラダにマッシュルームを入れたいと思います。 *Sarada ni masshu ruumu wo iretai to omoimasu.*
We would like to add mushrooms to the salad.

カーニバル (THE CARNIVAL)

1) 仮面 / マスク (mask)
かめん
kamen/masuku

2) 仮装 (costume/disguise)
かそう
kasou

3) フロート車 (float)
しゃ
furootosha

4) 花 (flowers)
はな
hana

5) スネアドラム (snare drum)
sunea doramu

6) ピエロ (clown)
piero

7) スーパーヒーロー (superhero)
suupaa hiiroo

8) プリンセス (princess)
purinsesu

9) 宇宙飛行士 (astronaut)
うちゅうひこうし
uchuu hikoushi

10) 物まね士 (mime)
もの　し
monomaneshi

11) 囚人 (prisoner)
しゅうじん
shuujin

12) 家電 (household appliance)
かでん
kaden

13) 妖精 (fairy)
ようせい
yousei

14) 木こり (lumberjack)
き
kikori

私はピエロが怖いです。*Watashi wa piero ga kowai desu.*
わたし　　　　　　　こわ
I am afraid of clowns.

病院ではマスクをつけなきゃいけません。*Byouin dewa masuku wo tsukenakya ikemasen.*
びょういん
You must wear a mask in the hospital.

父は私のスーパーヒーローでした。*Chichi wa watashi no suupaahiiroo deshita.*
ちち　わたし
My father was my superhero.

作業場 (THE WORKSHOP)

<small>さぎょうじょう</small>

1) 道具 (tool)
   dougu

2) 馬具 (saddlery)
   bagu

3) 大工仕事 (carpentry/woodwork)
   daiku shigoto

4) 椅子張り (upholstery/tapestry)
   isubari

5) 靴作り (shoemaking/shoerepair)
   kutsuzukuri

6) 銀細工 (silversmith)
   ginzaiku

7) 鍛冶屋 (blacksmith)
   kajiya

8) 自動車整備士 (mechanic)
   jidousha seibishi

9) 織物 (textile)
   orimono

10) パン屋 (bakery)
    panya

11) コスチュームジュエリー (costume jewelry)
    kosuchuumu juerii

12) 履物 (footwear)
    hakimono

13) メンテナンス (maintenance)
    mentenansu

14) 修理 (repair)
    shuuri

15) 絵画 / 絵 (painting)
    kaiga / e

16) ペイストリー (pastry)
    peisutorii

自動車整備士が私の車を修理し終えました。*Jidoushaseibishi ga watashino kuruma wo shuuri shioe mashita.*
The mechanic has finished repairing my car.

メンテナンスをしています。*Mentenansu wo shiteimasu.*
I am the maintenance guy.

あなたの絵を買いたいです。*Anata no e wo kaitai desu.*
I would like to buy your painting.

168

食料品店 (THE GROCERY STORE)
しょくりょうひんてん

1) パスタ (pasta)
   pasuta

2) お米 (rice)
   こめ
   okome

3) オーツ (oat)
   ootsu

4) パン (bread)
   pan

5) 油 (oils)
   あぶら
   abura

6) ソース (sauces)
   soosu

7) サラダドレッシング (salad dressings)
   sarada doresshingu

8) 調味料 (condiments)
   ちょうみりょう
   choumiryou

9) 缶詰め (canned goods)
   かんづ
   kanzume

10) ハム (ham)
    hamu

11) チーズ (cheese)
    chiizu

12) ピーナッツバター (peanut butter)
    piinattsu bataa

13) キャンディ (candy)
    kyandi

14) 豆 (beans)
    まめ
    mame

15) コーヒー (coffee)
    koohii

16) お茶 (tea)
    ちゃ
    ocha

ピーナッツバターサンドイッチが食べたい。 *Piinattsu bataa sandoicchi ga tabetai.*
た
I want to eat a peanut butter sandwich.

パンとお米、どっちが好き？ *Pan to okome, docchi ga suki ?*
こめ　　　　　す
Bread or rice, which do you like?

日本人は毎日お茶を飲みます。 *Nihon jin wa mainichi ocha wo nomimasu.*
にほんじん　まいにち　ちゃ　の
Japanese people drink green tea every day.

旅行 I (TRAVEL AND LIVING I)
りょこう

1) ツアーガイド (tour guide)
tsuaa gaido

2) 観光客 (tourist)
かんこうきゃく
kankoukyaku

3) 旅行者 (traveler)
りょこうしゃ
ryokousha

4) 荷物 (luggage)
にもつ
nimotsu

5) 手荷物 (hand luggage)
てにもつ
tenimotsu

6) カメラ (camera)
kamera

7) ホテル (hotel)
hoteru

8) ホステル (hostel)
hosuteru

9) ビーアンドビー (Bed & Breakfast/inn)
bii ando bii

10) 山小屋 (cabin)
やまごや
yamagoya

11) テント (tent)
tento

12) フライト (flight)
furaito

13) 出発 (departure)
しゅっぱつ
shuppatsu

14) 到着 (arrival)
とうちゃく
touchaku

ビーアンドビーで三泊予約しました。 *Bii ando bii de sanhaku yoyaku shimashita.*
さんはくよやく
I booked a bed and breakfast for three nights.

フライトは午後1時半出発です。 *Furaito wa gogo ichiji han shuppatsu desu.*
ごご じはんしゅっぱつ
The flight departs at 1:30 p.m.

カメラを忘れないで！ *Kamera wo wasurenaide!*
わす
Do not forget the camera!

旅行 II (TRAVEL AND LIVING II)

りょこう

1) 町 (town)
まち
machi

2) 地図 (map)
ちず
chizu

3) バス停 (bus stop)
てい
basutei

4) タクシー (taxi)
takushii

5) レンタカー会社 (car rental)
がいしゃ
rentakaa kaisha

6) 駅 (train station)
えき
eki

7) 空港 (airport)
くうこう
kuukou

8) パスポート (passport)
pasupooto

9) 身分証明書 (ID/identification card)
みぶんしょうめいしょ
mibun shoumeisho

10) 通過 (currency)
つうか
tsuuka

11) 現金 (cash)
げんきん
genkin

12) デビットカード (debit card)
debitto kaado

13) クレジットカード (credit card)
kurejitto kaado

14) 旅行ガイド (tourist guide)
りょこう
ryokou gaido

パスポートを更新しなきゃいけません。 *Pasupooto wo koushin shinakya ikemasen.*
こうしん
I must renew my passport.

デビットカードで支払いますか？現金で支払いますか？ *Debitto kaado de shiharaimasuka ?*
しはら　　　　げんきん　しはら
Genkin de shiharaimasuka ?
Are you paying by debit card or cash?

タクシーの予約をお願いできますか？ *Takushii no yoyaku wo onegai dekimasuka ?*
よやく　　　ねが
Could you book a taxi for me?

おもちゃ (TOYS)

1) ボール (ball)
   booru

2) テディベア (teddy bear)
   tedi bea

3) 電車 (train)
   でんしゃ
   densha

4) スケートボード (skateboard)
   sukeeto boodo

5) 人形 (doll)
   にんぎょう
   ningyou

6) レースカー (race car)
   reesu kaa

7) ロボット (robot)
   robotto

8) たこ (kite)
   tako

9) ドラム (drum)
   doramu

10) フラフープ (hula hoop)
   furafuupu

11) 手押し車 (wagon)
   てお　ぐるま
   teoshi guruma

12) ブロック (blocks)
   burokku

13) 木琴 (xylophone)
   もっきん
   mokkin

14) トラック (truck)
   torakku

15) 飛行機 (airplane)
   ひこうき
   hikouki

16) 積み木 (bricks)
   つ　き
   tsumiki

このロボットは日本製です。 *Kono robotto wa nihonsei desu.*
にほんせい
This robot is made in Japan.

私の娘がテディベアをなくしてしまいました。 *Watashi no musume ga tedi bea wo nakushite*
わたし　むすめ
shimaimashita.
My daughter has lost her teddy bear.

私にボールを投げて！ *Watashi ni booru wo nagete !*
わたし　　　　　な
Throw me the ball!

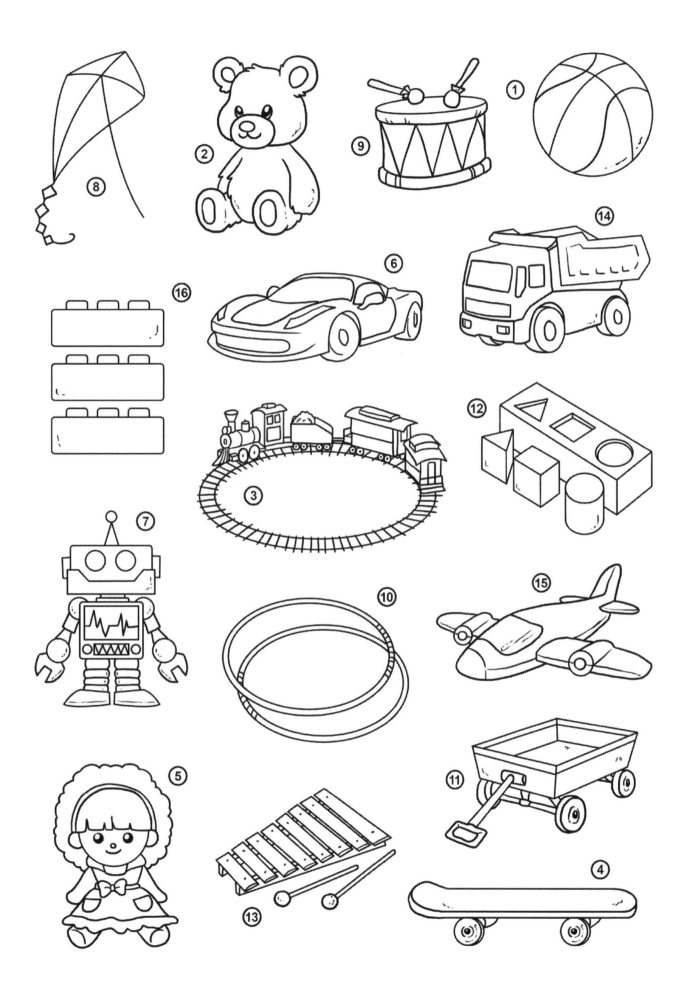

誕生日 (THE BIRTHDAY PARTY)

1) 誕生日バナー (birthday banner)
tanjoubi banaa

2) 飾りつけ (decoration)
kazaritsuke

3) プレゼント (present/gift)
purezento

4) 食器 (tableware)
shokki

5) 誕生日の人 (birthday person)
tanjoubi no hito

6) 風船 (balloon)
fuusen

7) バースデーケーキ (birthday cake)
baasudee keeki

8) お皿 (plates)
osara

9) フォーク (forks)
fooku

10) スプーン (spoons)
supuun

11) コップ (cups)
koppu

12) ストロー (straw)
sutoroo

13) ピニャータ (piñata)
pinyaata

14) ろうそく (candle)
rousoku

15) 帽子 (hat)
boushi

16) 招待客 / ゲスト (guests)
shoutai kyaku / gesuto

誕生日にたくさんのプレゼントをもらいました。 *Tanjoubi ni takusan no purezento wo moraimashita.*

I received a lot of gifts for my birthday.

バースデーケーキのろうそくを吹き消した。 *Baasudee keeki no rousoku wo fukikeshita.*
He blew out the candles on the birthday cake.

彼女は風船のアーチを作ってくれました。 *Kanojo wa fuusen no aachi wo tsukutte kuremashita.*
She made me a balloon arch.

反対の言葉 (OPPOSITES)

1) きれい (clean)
   kirei

2) 汚い (dirty)
   kitanai

3) 少ない (few)
   sukunai

4) 多い (many)
   ooi

5) 攻撃 (attack)
   kougeki

6) 防御 (defense)
   bougyo

7) まっすぐ (straight)
   massugu

8) 曲がった (curved)
   magatta

9) 一緒 (together)
   issho

10) 別々 (separated)
    betsubetsu

11) 若い (young)
    wakai

12) 老いた (old)
    oita

13) 裕福 (wealth)
    yuufuku

14) 不足 (shortage)
    fusoku

15) 凹型 (concave)
    ougata

16) 凸型 (convex)
    totsugata

私の両親はいつも一緒だ。*Watashi no ryoushin wa itsumo issho da.*
My parents are always together.

私が一番若い。*Watashi ga ichiban wakai.*
I am the youngest.

このお皿は汚い。*Kono osara wa kitanai.*
This plate is dirty.

QUIZ #8

Use arrows to match the corresponding translations:

a. arrival

b. cheese

c. teddy bear

d. tourist guide

e. map

f. forks

g. grass

h. candle

i. doll

j. airport

k. truck

l. flowers

m. tent

n. mask

o. rice

p. candy

1. テント

2. テディベア

3. 花
<small>はな</small>

4. 人形
<small>にんぎょう</small>

5. 地図
<small>ちず</small>

6. 空港
<small>くうこう</small>

7. キャンディ

8. トラック

9. ろうそく

10. 草
<small>くさ</small>

11. お米
<small>こめ</small>

12. チーズ

13. 到着
<small>とうちゃく</small>

14. フォーク

15. ツアーガイド

16. マスク

Fill in the blank spaces with the options below (use each word only once):

楽_{たの}しみにしていた日本旅行_{にほんりょこう}！＿＿＿＿＿に着_ついたら、カウンターで＿＿＿＿＿を見_みせてチェク

インをすませます。＿＿＿＿＿もカウンターにあずけました。私_{わたし}たちの＿＿＿＿＿は

のため少_{すこ}し遅_{おく}れていました。予定_{よてい}より少_{すこ}し遅_{おく}れて＿＿＿＿＿です。日本_{にほん}に＿＿＿＿＿したの

は夜_{よる}でした。

空港_{くうこう}につくと＿＿＿＿＿が待_まっていました。彼_{かれ}が準備_{じゅんび}した車_{くるま}で＿＿＿＿＿へ向_むかいました。

ホテルはとてもきれいでした。翌朝_{よくあさ}、＿＿＿＿＿を持_もって町_{まち}を歩_{ある}きました。東京_{とうきょう}は

本当_{ほんとう}に大_{おお}きな町_{まち}です！

空港_{くうこう}

メンテナンス

フライト

荷物_{にもつ}

出発_{しゅっぱつ}

パスポート

到着_{とうちゃく}

ツアーガイド

ホテル

地図_{ちず}

CONCLUSION

We would like to congratulate you on all the efforts you made to reach this point. Although there are certainly more things to learn in your Japanese language journey, this book has helped you to get familiar with some common Japanese vocabulary used in everyday life.

We have prepared a few tips that will help you continue your journey.

1. Study a little everyday

When it comes to the length of the study, studying a little every day is more effective than enduring painfully long but irregular study sessions. Take 30 minutes each day to learn Japanese. You will be very surprised with how much you will have progressed after a year!

2. Learn the correct pronunciation

Though Japanese people are very tolerant and will most probably be pleased to see your efforts to speak Japanese, a heavy accent however may be distracting from what you really want to say. So, give attention to proper pronunciation right from the start! This will prevent you from forming bad habits. One of the key ways to master proper pronunciation is listening to spoken Japanese. Take advantage of Japanese movies, songs and TV shows. Listen carefully and write down what you hear even if you do not understand the whole context. Then use a dictionary to make sure the meaning.

3. Use what you have learned

The language acquisition journey can be compared to swimming. You cannot learn to swim just by reading a book. You have to get into the water! Likewise, you cannot learn a language just from grammar books. You need to actually interact with Japanese people! But this doesn't necessarily mean that you have to move to Japan. Thanks to technology, there are many ways to interact with native Japanese speakers.

4. Understanding the culture

Learning a language is also learning a new culture. Watch Japanese movies, go to Japanese restaurants and read Japanese books. Try to learn not just the language but the culture.

5. Don't be afraid of making mistakes

Mistakes are part of the learning process. Don't expect perfection from yourself. It may not be wise to compare your progress with others. And lastly keep your sense of humor and laugh at your mistakes!

After all, learning a foreign language is a lifelong pursuit. Therefore, even if your progress seems slow, don't be discouraged! Enjoy each step of the journey!

ANSWERS

QUIZ #1

a-4.　b-7.　c-9.　d-5.　e-2.　f-13.　g-6.　h-16.　i-15.　j-1.　k-14.　l-3.
m-10.　n-11.　o-12.　p-8.

わたしの<ruby>彼女<rt>かのじょ</rt></ruby>は２７<ruby>才<rt>さい</rt></ruby>です。わたしたちは３<ruby>年<rt>ねん</rt></ruby><ruby>前<rt>まえ</rt></ruby>に、<ruby>日本<rt>にほん</rt></ruby>で<ruby>会<rt>あ</rt></ruby>いました。<ruby>彼女<rt>かのじょ</rt></ruby>の<ruby>性格<rt>せいかく</rt></ruby>はとても<ruby>親切<rt>しんせつ</rt></ruby>で、<ruby>真面目<rt>まじめ</rt></ruby>です。<ruby>目<rt>め</rt></ruby>が<ruby>大<rt>おお</rt></ruby>きくて、<ruby>髪の毛<rt>かみけ</rt></ruby>が<ruby>短<rt>みじか</rt></ruby>いです。<ruby>動物<rt>どうぶつ</rt></ruby>が<ruby>大好<rt>だいす</rt></ruby>きで、<ruby>猫<rt>ねこ</rt></ruby>を<ruby>飼<rt>か</rt></ruby>っています。<ruby>昨日<rt>きのう</rt></ruby>は<ruby>友達<rt>ともだち</rt></ruby>をさそって、みんなで<ruby>動物園<rt>どうぶつえん</rt></ruby>に<ruby>行<rt>い</rt></ruby>きました。ゾウはとても<ruby>大<rt>おお</rt></ruby>きいので、<ruby>人気<rt>にんき</rt></ruby>があります。<ruby>彼女<rt>かのじょ</rt></ruby>の<ruby>兄弟<rt>きょうだい</rt></ruby>は３０<ruby>才<rt>さい</rt></ruby>で、<ruby>今<rt>いま</rt></ruby>ニューヨークに<ruby>住<rt>す</rt></ruby>んでいます。<ruby>彼女<rt>かのじょ</rt></ruby>のお<ruby>父<rt>とう</rt></ruby>さんは６０<ruby>才<rt>さい</rt></ruby>で、シカゴに<ruby>住<rt>す</rt></ruby>んでいます。

QUIZ # 2

a-7.　b-1.　c-9.　d-16.　e-15.　f-13.　g-2.　h-10.　i-14.　j-6.　k-12.　l-11.
m-8.　n-3.　o-5.　p-4.

サンディは<ruby>英語<rt>えいご</rt></ruby>の<ruby>先生<rt>せんせい</rt></ruby>です。<ruby>日曜日<rt>にちようび</rt></ruby>に、<ruby>夫<rt>おっと</rt></ruby>とハイキングに<ruby>行<rt>い</rt></ruby>きました。<ruby>天気予報<rt>てんきよほう</rt></ruby>は<ruby>雨<rt>あめ</rt></ruby>だったのでレインコートを<ruby>持<rt>も</rt></ruby>っていきました。<ruby>朝<rt>あさ</rt></ruby>は<ruby>晴<rt>は</rt></ruby>れていて、<ruby>暖<rt>あたた</rt></ruby>かい<ruby>一日<rt>いちにち</rt></ruby>でした。<ruby>日差<rt>ひざ</rt></ruby>しが<ruby>強<rt>つよ</rt></ruby>かったので、<ruby>帽子<rt>ぼうし</rt></ruby>をかぶり<ruby>日焼<rt>ひや</rt></ruby>け<ruby>止<rt>ど</rt></ruby>めを<ruby>塗<rt>ぬ</rt></ruby>りました。<ruby>山<rt>やま</rt></ruby>の<ruby>中<rt>なか</rt></ruby>でリスをみつけました。きれいなチョウもたくさん<ruby>飛<rt>と</rt></ruby>んでいました。でも、<ruby>蚊<rt>か</rt></ruby>も<ruby>多<rt>おお</rt></ruby>くて、<ruby>虫<rt>むし</rt></ruby>よけを<ruby>持<rt>も</rt></ruby>ってくればよかったと<ruby>思<rt>おも</rt></ruby>いました。

QUIZ # 3

a-2.　b-3.　c-1.　d-8.　e-9.　f-13.　g-11.　h-4.　i-12.　j-15.　k-5.　l-6.
m-16.　n-7.　o-10　p-14.

これが私の家です。最近壁を黄色に塗りました。裏庭には大きな木があります。
秋になると紅葉がとてもきれいです。でも、落ち葉を集めるのはたいへんです。冬の寒
い日には、バルコニーでココアを飲むのが好きです。雪が降れば、弟と雪玉を作って
遊びます。リビングルームの暖炉に火をつけて、ソファーで本を読むのも大好きです。
日曜日はみんなでテレビを見ます。

QUIZ # 4

a-15.　b-13.　c-11.　d-9.　e-7.　f-5.　g-3.　h-1.　i-16.　j-14.　k-10.　l-2.
m-4.　n-6.　o-8.　p-12.

アンドリューはITエンジニアです。シカゴのオフィスで働いていて、上司からも信頼
されています。パソコンにくわしく、壊れたらすぐに直してくれます。休日は、旅行
するのが大好きです。クルーズ船に乗ってカリブ海を旅したり、飛行機で日本に行ったり
しました。イタリアのローマで見た遺跡はすばらしいと言っていました。自然が大好きで、
友達と山に登ったり、川で泳ぐこともあります。スポーツも得意で、日曜日は
毎週バスケットボールをしています。でも寒いのが苦手で、スキーやアイススケートは
あまりしません。

QUIZ # 5

a-7.　b-8.　c-6.　d-11.　e-2.　f-12.　g-1.　h-3.　i-4.　j-13.　k-5.　l-9.
m-10.　n-16.　o-14.　p-15.

私のおじいちゃんは農家をしています。牛や羊をたくさん飼っています。またたまね
ぎやじゃがいもなどの野菜も育てています。私は毎年夏に遊びに行って、乳搾りを
したり牛小屋のそうじを手伝います。田舎なので、空気もきれいです。夜は流れ星が見

えることもあります。夜はお茶を飲みながら、アコースティック・ギターを弾いてくれます。でも去年は病気になり、一度救急車で病院へ運ばれて、手術を受けました。今でもときどきお医者さんに行きますが、すっかりよくなりました。

QUIZ # 6

a-11.　b-7.　c-9.　d-3.　e-8.　f-2.　g-1.　h-16.　i-15.　j-5.　k-6.　l-14.
m-10.　n-4.　o-13.　p-12.

高校の卒業式のあと、家族と遊園地にいきました。弟と私はメリーゴーランドに乗りました。おかあさんは高いところが苦手なのでおとうさんとローラーコースターに乗りました。お昼ごはんはチーズバーガーを食べました。おかあさんはベジタリアンなのでシーザーサラダを食べていました。来月は大学に入ります。おかあさんは私に「大学でなにをしたいの？」と聞きました。私は「世界中を旅行する」と答えました。みんな笑っていました。でも本気なんです。お金を稼いだり、起業家になることにはあまり興味がありません。旅の途中で外国人の女の子と結婚するかも！

QUIZ # 7

a-1.　b-7.　c-2.　d-8.　e-12.　f-3.　g-4.　h-10.　i-16.　j-15.　k-5.　l-9.
m-6.　n-11.　o-14.　p-13.

昨日サンディと一緒に新しいレストランに行きました。地下鉄に乗って１０分ほどの場所です。大きな広場の前にあります。レストランの椅子は柔らかく、とても快適でした。まずはウェイターを呼んで、ワインを注文しました。メインコースはビーフステーキです。デザートにチーズケーキを食べました。とてもおいしかったです。良いサービスだったのでチップをたくさん払いました。そのあと、二人で町をすこし歩きました。

QUIZ # 8

a-13.　b-12.　c-2.　d-15.　e-5.　f-14.　g-10.　h-9.　i-4.　j-6.　k-8.　l-3.
m-1.　n-16.　o-11.　p-7.

楽しみにしていた日本旅行！空港に着いたら、カウンターでパスポートを見せてチェクインをすませます。荷物もカウンターにあずけました。私たちのフライトはメンテナンスのため少し遅れていました。予定より少し遅れて出発です。日本に到着したのは夜でした。空港につくとツアーガイドが待っていました。彼が準備した車でホテルへ向かいました。ホテルはとてもきれいでした。翌朝、地図を持って町を歩きました。東京は本当に大きな町です！

MORE BOOKS BY LINGO MASTERY

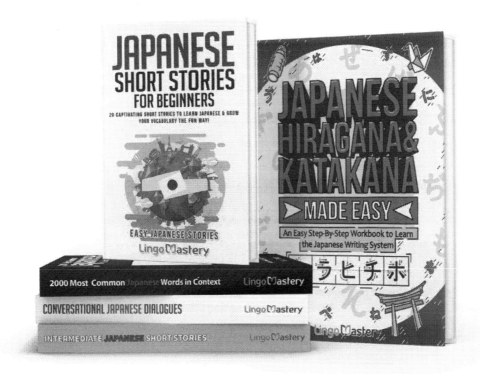

We are not done teaching you Japanese until you're fluent!

Here are some other titles you might find useful in your journey of mastering Japanese:

- **Japanese Short Stories for Beginners**
- **Japanese Hiragana & Katakana Made Easy**
- **2000 Most Common Japanese Words in Context**
- **Conversational Japanese Dialogues**

But we got many more!

Check out all our titles at www.LingoMastery.com/Japanese

Made in United States
Orlando, FL
17 February 2023

30100497R00109